Effective
Access to
INFORMATION

TODAY'S CHALLENGE,
TOMORROW'S OPPORTUNITY

Effective Access to

INFORMATION

TODAY'S CHALLENGE, TOMORROW'S OPPORTUNITY

ALPHONSE F. TREZZA, Editor

A CONFERENCE SPONSORED BY THE FLORIDA STATE UNIVERSITY SCHOOL OF LIBRARY AND INFORMATION STUDIES AND THE CENTER FOR PROFESSIONAL DEVELOPMENT AND PUBLIC SERVICE

G. K. Hall & Co.
Boston

Effective Access to Information:
Today's Challenge, Tomorrow's Opportunity

Alphonse F. Trezza, editor

Copyright 1989
by G.K. Hall & Co.
70 Lincoln Street
Boston, MA 02111

Printed on acid-free paper and bound
in The United States of America.

Library of Congress Cataloging-in-Publication Data

Effective access to information : today's challenge, tomorrow's opportunity:
    a conference / sponsored by the Florida State University School of Library
    and Information Studies and the Center for Professional Development and
    Public Service ; Alphonse F. Trezza, editor.
        p. cm. -- (Professional librarian series)
    Papers originally presented at the Sixth Annual Florida State
University Library Conference, held in Tallahassee, Mar. 6-9, 1988.
    Bibliography: p.
    ISBN 0-8161-1910-4 (pbk.)
    1. Information services--Congresses. 2. Freedom of information-
-Congresses. 3. Government information--Congresses. 4. Information
technology--Congresses. 5. Library science--Technological
innovations--Congresses. I. Trezza, Alphonse F. II. Florida State
University. School of Library and Information Studies.
III. Florida State University. Center for Professional Development
and Public Service. IV. Florida State University Library Conference
(6th : 1988 : Tallahassee, Fla.) V. Series.
Z674.2.E37 1989
025.5'2--dc20   89-32914
                                                                    CIP

Contents

Preface

What roles should the government and private sector play in the collection, production, and dissemination of information? What impact will the proliferation of information in electronic format have on access and every citizen's right to know? How do we resolve the contradictions that exist between the philosophical ideal of free access and the political and economic realities facing libraries?

These were some of the difficult and complex questions addressed during the sixth annual Florida State University Library Conference, "Effective Access to Information: Today's Challenge, Tomorrow's Opportunity," held in Tallahassee, 6-9 March 1988. Conference chairperson Alphonse F. Trezza brought together an impressive list of distinguished speakers from government, academe, the information industry, and the library profession, to discuss one of the most controversial and important issues facing information professionals today.

F. William Summers, dean of FSU School of Library and Information Studies and President-Elect of ALA, delivered the keynote address, "The Need to Know." Summers openly and frankly spelled out the various concerns involved regarding access to information and every citizen's right to be informed. He spoke of the philosophy of James Madison and George Mason, of the social contract between people and their government in this country, and the freedom to know that is embedded in the logic and spirit of the Constitution. That freedom is being assaulted, according to Summers, on several fronts in today's society.

Summers asserted that the information policies of the federal government endanger the availability of and our access to information by and about the U.S. government. The growth of the Office of Management and Budget as the "information czar" of the country and its reliance on cost-benefit analyses and cost-recovery requirements pose serious threats to our freedom to know. Privatization and the concentration of more information in fewer hands is, in Summers's view, creating an information oligopoly. Government must encourage competition and diversity while keeping the information needs of all citizens in mind. There is a difficulty when certain information areas are not served adequately by the private sector, and when the government is eliminating much of what it has traditionally provided while charging more for what it continues to provide.

Summers pointed to the National Technical Information Service (NTIS) as one of the few information-providing successes of government, providing scientific and technical information in a cost-effective manner. Now NTIS is threatened by the possibility of privatization. Summers questioned the wisdom in placing so much publicly-supported information into private hands and relegating government to publishing only unprofitable information while leaving the revenue-providing information in the hands of industry. The Government Printing Office has also undertaken a feasibility study to examine the possible privatization of its distribution system. Contracting out federal library services under the provisions of OMB Circular A-76 was cited as another example where the economic management of resources was placed above the information needs of citizens. Placing these information services into private--and possibly foreign--hands could severely limit access to needed government information.

Summers noted other threats to our freedom of access, including the efforts of private groups to censor materials, particularly in the public schools; the problem of dealing with the overwhelming mass of data that already is available and that continues to grow; and economic and budget concerns that hold information hostage to our ability to pay.

In concluding his address, Summers stated that while privatization may be efficient, it also discriminates against those unable to pay. He accepted that public access may be inefficient, but it is the fairest means of ensuring that the information needs of every citizen are equitably considered. He suggested that we might adapt the same attitude toward information as that which seems to be developing toward universal health care in this country: that medical services should be available to those who need them, regardless of the individual's ability to pay. Summers believes it is an ideal that demands our commitment and cooperation if it is to be realized.

The Government's Philosophy and Practice

The second general session of the conference examined the federal government's philosophy and practice regarding information access. J. Timothy Sprehe, senior policy analyst of OMB's Office of Information and Regulatory Affairs and principal author of OMB Circular A-130, "Management of Federal Information Resources," addressed the role of the Office of Management and Budget. Sprehe described the agency's work as satisfying the mandate of the Paperwork Reduction Act to minimize the paperwork and cost burden on the public and to provide regulations for the collection and publication of government information. Circular A-130, according to Sprehe, attempts to cover the entire life cycle of information by also presenting guidelines for information dissemination, though the original act says little about dissemination. Sprehe acknowledged that the library community had a very influential role in the drafting of the circular. He reported that a revision of A-130 is currently underway and is expected to be completed by the end of the fiscal year. Information policies regarding electronic databases will be among the topics addressed in the revised circular.

Bernadine A. Hoduski, professional staff member for library and distribution services of the Joint Committee on Printing, spoke of the Congressional role in information policy development. She stated that policies are being made every day, as the three branches of government compete for control over the collection and publication of information. Congress, according to Hoduski, has traditionally been supportive of research and the collection and dissemination of information, one motivating reason being that Congress is a major consumer of information. Hoduski believes that libraries--especially federal libraries and the Depository Library System--are the logical place for the exchange and dissemination of information and can serve as a vehicle for information sharing among the branches of government. She sees the handling and dissemination of electronic information as the most critical issue facing information professionals today.

Talbot (Sandy) D'Alemberte, dean of the Florida State University College of Law, concluded this session of the conference by looking at the role of the courts. He spoke of the complexity of our system of government--the three branches on both the state and federal levels--and observed that the judicial branch has traditionally been the most open. He stated that the courts see their role as interpreting the policies of the other branches and have generally protected the public's right of access to information. D'Alemberte contrasted the American experience with the British Officials Secrets Act, where embarrassing and injurious information can be restricted by governmental fiat. States have had a better record protecting the public's right to know than the federal government, he said, and state courts have given the issue higher priority than their federal counterparts. The reason may be the supervisory or administrative role courts play in access cases and the struggle they have had with the extension of a full constitutional right to access of information. Dean D'Alemberte spoke from notes and did not prepare a paper for the proceedings; his comments on the role of the courts are thus not in this volume. Suggestions for reading on this topic are found in the bibliography at the end of the volume.

The Private Sector's Philosophy and Role

The philosophy and role of the private sector in information access was the focus of the third general session. Paul G. Zurkowski, president of the Information Industry Association, opened the session by presenting the view from the information industry. He believes that, as an information community, we must first decide where we want to go and how we are going to get there. He reviewed the advances in information technology and presented a map of the information industry today. He pointed out that the forms of information are clearly multidimensional and that no single policy for handling information will suffice. Zurkowski said that information businesses and libraries have common goals and concerns and that if the true mind-expanding potential of information is to be successfully tapped we must all work together. He called for a Carnegie-like initiative to join the efforts of the public and private sectors to address how we might fully utilize America's information wealth.

Richard R. Rowe, president of the Faxon Company, reemphasized the importance of a clear vision of purpose and direction in the development of information policy. In presenting the view from the entrepreneur, he observed that a sense of confusion and mistrust exists between libraries and information entrepreneurs and outlined the possible barriers to meaningful discussion and progress. He suggested that we work to develop a new theory or taxonomy of information, in an effort to reach a common understanding. Rowe saw information poverty in society as our greatest challenge, citing the forecast that the current generation of children in elementary school will be the first generation in this country's history to be less well educated than their parents. He sees new technologies as offering opportunities for advancing toward our common goals. The construction of a global fiber-optic network and the concept of a personalized, artificial-intelligence based workstation (or knowledge navigator) are developments that have much potential for making information more accessible and better utilized.

Robert Hayes, dean of the Graduate School of Library and Information Science at UCLA, concluded this session by examining access from the profession's point of view. He defined the private sector as nongovernmental organizations whose primary support comes from the sale of information and whose policies and decisions are based on the marketplace. The professional imperatives of libraries, on the other hand, include preservation of the record and providing free and open access to the record. He added that these imperatives are not absolute and are sometimes constrained by economic realities. Hayes sees the major roles of the private sector as a source of publication--from the identification of potential publications to their packaging, marketing, and distribution--and as a value-added processor--producing access tools, analyses, and other information services. Hayes noted the issues that separate libraries from the private sector, including pricing, copyright, and the privatization of government information. He also pointed out the interdependency and shared interests of the two sides. He challenged the information profession to bear in mind the common view that information is important and valuable to society and to work toward making this partnership successful.

The Librarian and Information Specialist View

The fourth general session of the conference presented views on information access from the perspective of the librarian and information specialist. Stephen M. Hayes, associate librarian for Reference and Public Documents at Notre Dame University and Chair of ALA-GODORT, led off this session by talking about the government documents depository system. He reviewed the history of the depository program, pointing out that the role and function of the program has never been clearly defined. He stated that, while all depositories act with the general mission to make government information accessible to the public, the diversity of the needs, scope, and focus of the various libraries and the absence of clear direction cause problems for the depository community and create a lack of cohesiveness. Hayes objected to the Reagan administration's efforts to decrease the collection, publication, and dissemination of government information. He questioned the role of the OMB, citing a case where the agency instructed the Bureau of the Census in how large the census should be, the size of statistical samples, and, in some cases, which questions should be asked. In his own experience at Notre Dame, the library has noticed a 25 percent decrease in government information resources. Hayes sees the issue of privatization as the biggest problem today. He believes the government has a minimum obligation to provide a safety net of information resources at no cost for those who cannot afford private sector information products.

William DeJohn, director of MINITEX, spoke of the role of networks in information access. He defined the library network as a formal structure organized to facilitate, exchange, transfer, and develop new services through cooperative membership agreements. He observed that resource sharing and networking is revolutionizing access to information. The challenges that lie ahead include training staff and users to cope with the avalanche of new technology and information, designing communication links between local area networks, and developing regional and national document delivery systems. DeJohn stated that while resource sharing is an effective means to access needed information, it still is not a substitute for direct, on-site access necessary to meet the majority of user questions and needs.

John N. Berry, III, editor of *Library Journal,* closed this session by addressing the fee or free dilemma. Berry drew from the reasoning of Thomas Jefferson and Adam Smith in presenting the precepts of his defense for free library services: (1) that government is best that governs least and (2) that government must not interfere unless the marketplace fails. He stated that the current debate over the provision of information services is confined to what constitutes market failure. Berry traced the history of the development of public libraries in this country and affirmed the establishment of publicly supported libraries as a common good. He sees the attachment of user fees to library services as dangerous and believes that libraries are as worthy of full payment by government as any other public service. Current library services are a bargain, according to Berry, serving 35-40 percent of the population with only about 1 percent of tax revenues. He refuted the arguments for imposing user fees, stating that they discourage information use, are discriminatory, and send the wrong message about the nature and value of information. All of society benefits when any one of us takes advantage of library services. He believes that we cannot depend on the marketplace to develop and maintain an informed citizenry. The library, in Berry's eyes, is a democratic institution, comparable to the lighthouse. It protects the public good of information and should be there for all to use freely in times of need.

The Needs of the Many Publics

Warren J. Haas, president of the Council on Library Resources, delivered the Samuel Lazerow Memorial Lecture. He addressed the needs of the many publics in "Scholars, Youth, and the General Public." Haas said that user expectations of library services are not being met because libraries are operated by management priorities rather than a focus on user needs. He described conflict, especially in academic and research libraries, between user expectations and the limitations of technology, resource sharing, and financing. In meeting these expectations, librarians are asked to turn the impossible into routine procedure. Haas further observed that information itself must be understood and that the public must rethink its priorities. He concluded with the warning that unless user needs and budgets are brought into balance, the information revolution will be lost.

Removing or Neutralizing Barriers

The final session of the conference explored the various barriers to access of information. Jane Heiser, administrator of the Office of Life-Long Learning at the Enoch Pratt Free Library in Baltimore, talked about the problems of illiteracy, which she considers the greatest and most serious barrier to access. She described the enormity of the problem in the United States and explained the differences between functional and cultural illiteracy. She also defined aliteracy, noting that one-fourth of the population can but does not read and may lose reading as a skill through non-use. Heiser implored the need for pluralistic, community-based programs to help address the problems of illiteracy. She remarked that libraries have been involved in efforts concerning illiteracy and aliteracy all along, yet we lack the organization and coordination to effectively deal with the issue.

S. Michael Malinconico, dean of the School of Computer, Information, and Library Sciences at the Pratt Institute, spoke on the use of technology as a tool for making libraries more accessible. He discussed the various physical, conceptual, and fiscal barriers to libraries. New technologies, including user friendly search systems and catalogs, expert systems, and data point technology, offer exciting potential in helping make libraries more accessible. Malinconico believes that the possibility of a truly comprehensive integrated library system, while desirable, is an unrealistic and impractical goal. Instead, the development of standards that would permit several systems to interface and achieve comprehensive integration is a challenging and more likely objective. Malinconico also remarked that we need to be sensitive to the new barriers created by introducing new technologies into libraries.

Leigh Estabrook, dean of the School of Library and Information Science, University of Illinois at Urbana-Champagne, delivered the final paper of the conference. Estabrook examined the contradictions that exist between the stated ideal of total and equal access and the practical realities we face every day. In this Darwinian struggle, librarians end up compromising certain philosophical beliefs in making political and economic choices. She distinguished among the library as an institution, librarianship as a profession, and the practice of librarianship to demonstrate the differing goals of each. Estabrook expressed the need for a moral philosophy among librarians, incorporating the values of justice, courage, and honesty. She stated that we have a moral obligation to keep pushing the boundaries of access and to support one another individually in the struggle to achieve our goals. Estabrook concluded her presentation by quoting from a student's comments on why he chose librarianship as a profession: "Because providing information to people who want it is a good thing to do; because libraries do not pollute, do not destroy, do not attempt to create wealth out of nothing; because I am convinced that many people do not have access to information; because I can justify libraries on moral and ethical grounds; and because I like to read and find things out."

This year's FSU Library Conference brought over 130 participants from 19 states together for four days to listen, learn, discuss, and argue about the various issues involved in providing effective access to information. The experience proved to be an informative and thought-provoking one for many of the delegates present. The topic will continue to be a formidable challenge to the entire information community.

DANIEL P. O'MAHONY
School of Library and Information Studies
Florida State University

DAVID M. JONES
School of Library and Information Studies
Florida State University

DAVID M. STRICKLER
School of Library and Information Studies
Florida State University

ALPHONSE F. TREZZA
Conference Chair
School of Library and Information Studies
Florida State University

Acknowledgments

The success of any conference is due to the work and support of many people. The encouragement and support of F. William Summers, dean of the School of Library and Information Studies, as well as the faculty and students contributed greatly to the professional excellence of the conference. The physical facilities, the arrangements, and the meals are essential to a smoothly run, enjoyable meeting. The credit for this goes to the director, Mary L. Pankowski, and the staff of the Center for Professional Development and Public Service at Florida State University.

It would have been impossible to plan and implement not only the 1988 conference but the previous five without the patience, understanding, support, and love of my wife Mildred. I dedicate these proceedings and future conferences to her.

Introduction: The Need to Know

F. WILLIAM SUMMERS

Dean, School of Library and Information Studies
Florida State University
Tallahassee, Florida

I first encountered the term *need to know* in some dark black-and-white World War II movie, when one character in a military uniform asked a question and the another said solemnly, "That is on a need to know basis." I encountered the term again in a stint as a cryptographer in the navy in training programs dealing with handling classified material. Until very recently, whenever I thought of the concept of *need to know* it was in the military context that suggests that the fewer people who know something the better, and certainly that only those whose duties specifically require them to know something should know it. Because I had encountered the concept in the context of military defense, I never questioned its validity or analyzed the degree to which it conflicts with our basic democratic principals of free inquiry and full citizen access to information by and about the activities of their national, state, and local governments.

It was not until the term *national security* came to be used as a shield to protect a wide variety of illegal acts, both civil and criminal, that many of us began to question the validity of the concept and to recognize that while militarily very appropriate in times of war, it was essentially an undemocratic and nonegalitarian concept that ill suited our national purposes and character.

In addition to this viewpoint, one can also think of the *need to know*, as one of those basic human needs that we all must satisfy and that we spend our lives trying to meet. In that context, the need to know takes on a different

1

set of meanings and drives a different set of human behaviors. In this sense those things that frustrate our need to know become serious obstacles that we must try to overcome, and consistent failure to overcome them can result in injury to our intellectual or emotional system. Viewed in this light the person who gives up on the library because it is inflexible or unfriendly is not just a lost opportunity for service, but a casualty and a person whose human needs are either unmet or diminished. We know from other areas of human study that the failure to have one's basic needs met causes changes in emotional health that may have a long-term consequence. There is no assertion here that information deprivation leads to mental illness or antisocial behavior, but neither should we too quickly dismiss such a possibility from consideration. We simply do not know very much about the strength of the needs to know in humans or the consequences of frustration of that need.

There are, however, some things about the need to know that we as a people believe, and those beliefs shape our behavior just as surely as if they were scientifically established fact.

Let us briefly examine some of these basic beliefs that shape our system of societal values in terms of both human and organizational behavior:

1. We believe that the need to know and the freedom to know are at the root of what Rousseau called the social contract that binds and holds us together as a society. It is reflected in that basic body of law we call the Constitution. Recent study of the history of our Constitution leads me to believe that the right to know, though not specifically enumerated there is nevertheless deeply imbedded in the logic of the Constitution because of the thinking of two men, both from Virginia, James Madison and George Mason. Madison believed that the more people who were brought into the system on a free and equal basis, the safer are the liberties and lives of all of us. Mason insisted that the constitution must have a strong and clear bill of rights because he distrusted politicians and wanted to empower the people with rights to protect themselves against excessive and invasive government. Our freedom to know is reflected and implied in many places in the constitution.

2. Copyright, which many people are now attempting to assert as a restriction on the right to know, exists "to promote the progress of science and the useful arts." We do not have copyright for the purpose of enriching authors, or data-base vendors. We do not have copyright to create a marketplace in which the government can turn over to private vendors the results of its data collections and deliberations in order that those vendors can make a profit.

2

Copyright exists to ensure that citizens can meet their needs to know and that our society, not the copyright holders, will be enriched. We must recognize that there is a clear and very real antagonism between the goals of libraries and those of copyright holders. Libraries exist to make information as widely available as possible, copyright holders prefer that every use of a copyright item result from a purchase of something with a royalty to the copyright holder. There are already on the drawing boards "pay-per-use" systems that would monitor the usage of information and make charges either directly to users or to their library surrogates, for each use made. We must remember that the copyright holder can market the information in any kind of marketplace he or she chooses and on whatever terms that marketplace will bear. A recent report commissioned by the Information Industry Association identified the following in one of its scenarios for the future: "public libraries flourish as they foster new CD ROM based, pay-peruse approaches that adequately compensate authors and publishers and make massive amounts of information widely available." It seems that we citizens who want to have our need to know met are caught between the Scylla of the marketplace and the Charybdis of expecting the government to protect our basic rights. Truly a disturbing choice that must make us all yearn for a third alternative.

In addition the Information Industry Association quote has some other very serious flaws with which we need to be concerned. First, it assumes that authors and publishers are not now adequately compensated and further that only pay-per-use approaches have the capacity to make massive amounts of information available, a statement that ignores the fact that we have had rapidly expanding information availability for many, many years without a highly structured and profit-oriented marketplace. The quote deftly skirts the problem that is highly evident in the one truly market-driven information service we have available--television. Mass-market television has produced a deterioration in the quality of programming not only in our broadcasting but in the movie markets, which are television driven. Book publishing is also increasingly television determined. If we commit our information services solely to market-driven forces we can expect the same deterioration. Who wants to live in a society guided by the information delivery equivalent of "Laverne and Shirley?"

3. Another of the principles that have until recently governed the need to know in our society relates to the creation and distribution of information by the U.S. government. We have believed that when the government creates information it has a duty to make that information available to citizens who may find it useful or indeed who are simply curious. We also believe that government should make this information available to citizens at the lowest possible cost or even on a subsidized basis if it is important. We have seen a serous eroding of that principal in recent years and that erosion has turned into a virtual landslide in the last 6 years under the Reagan administration. Since 1982 one out of every four of the government's 16,000 publications has been eliminated.

How Fares the Need to Know Today?

With these principles as a framework let us examine how the need to know fares in today's society. Is our need to know better or worse met today than it has been in the past? What does the future look like if present trends with respect to our access to knowledge continue?

Information by and about the U.S. Government

That heading comes from a chronology of events that the American Library Association's Washington office has been issuing for the past six years in an effort to review what it considers serious interruptions in the citizen's right to know about the activities of government.

OMB as Information Controller

Perhaps the most serious problem we face is the development of the Office of Management and Budget as the major controlling force on the creation and availability of information from the government. Clearly no one believes or perhaps ever intended that the OMB would be the information czar in this country but it has become just that. Using powers granted to it by the Paperwork Reduction Act of 1980, the implementation of the Grace Commission recommendations, and the power to control agency budgets, the OMB has acted to curtail drastically access to government information.

These powers are wide ranging. A few examples: The U.S. Census Bureau believes that the 1990 census will require a sample of 16 million households; the OMB wants a sample of only 10 million. Given the kinds of decisions we make all through our society in the public as well as the private sectors of the economy can we leave the determination of the statistical validity of our census to the bean counters? Through its Circular A-130

Management of Federal Information Resources, the OMB requires cost-benefit analysis of government information activities, maximum reliance on the private sector, and cost recovery through user charges.

While the private sector bemoans the "unfair competition" of government information services we need to be very aware of the concentration of private information in fewer and fewer hands. In 1958, for example, 72 percent of all books were sold by independent one-store firms, today 52 percent are sold by four large bookstore chains. *Five, repeat five* database vendors account for over 90 percent of the sales and uses of database services in this country. Nine firms account for 50 percent of all trade book sales. Increasingly the information marketplace is shifting away from competition and toward oligarchy--and not just domestic oligarchy, but international conglomerates that own both hardware and software publishers, computer companies, data processing services, motion picture companies, theaters, television networks, newspapers, and other information companies. We cannot afford a worldwide cartel of information producers anymore than we can afford a worldwide cartel of petroleum producers. Government policy must be to increase healthy and socially responsible competition in the information marketplace, not competition for its own sake. We have already seen that getting the government out of the airline business has resulted in a deterioration of airline service for most communities and over concentrations of service for the heaviest markets. You may have noticed this phenomenon at work in your efforts to reach this conference. We cannot permit the same policy in information services.

Elimination of Government Publications

Does it really matter if the government ceases to publish its little pamphlet, *Your Healthy Baby,* the all-time best seller? Probably not. There are many popular books and pamphlets available at a very reasonable cost that can convey the same information. The real problem may be how the government decides which publications to eliminate and what forces shape such a decision. A decision to eliminate information that the private sector has already provided at reasonable cost is one thing, but the decision to eliminate government information in the hope or naive belief that the private market will automatically make it available is quite another. Let me list a few publications that the government has recently abandoned: *Psychopharmacology Abstracts, Oil Pollution Abstracts,* and *Pesticides Abstracts.* Try getting those in your nearby B. Dalton's. In addition, the cost of a subscription to the *Congressional Record,* the journal of our government, has gone from $75 to $208 and the *Monthly Catalog* of government publications, the basic bibliography of government information has gone from $65 to $215. Not only is the government eliminating publications, it is making it very expensive to learn about those that remain.

5

Privatization of Government Information

Perhaps the most far-reaching and frightening of the government's so-called efficiencies are its efforts to turn over to private publication and operation many of its basic information collection and dissemination activities. No example more clearly demonstrates the dangerous implications of this trend than the Reagan administration's plan to privatize the National Technical Information Service.

NTIS was established to make available at reasonable cost technical reports resulting from research and contract work done for the government. These reports are essential to government contractors and to private and public researchers in most of the technical fields. The NTIS has been one of the rare success stories in government. It is entirely self-sufficient. It operates without government subsidy and more than pays its own costs, at the same time delivering high-quality service to its users. What is to be made of the administration's desire to convert this service to a private enterprise and take it outside of the government to operate as profit-making enterprise? Are we really prepared to have our basic technical information agency operated as a subsidiary of some foreign owned corporation? If you think that this example is far fetched, consider that the principal critic of the National Library of Medicine's publication, *Index Medicus*, is Elsevier North Holland, an internationally owned company that wants the United States to either discontinue these publications or raise the price about five fold because it considers the NLM publications to be competitive with its own. For many years we have heard the criticism that government needs to be more businesslike. None of these criticisms was more strident than those from the Reagan administration. NTIS is a perfect example of government being more businesslike and now we are to get it out of government. Is it really sound national policy that the government will publish only those things that are inefficient and uneconomical and everything else be given over to private sources? It must also be emphasized that the private vendors do not want the entire job. They do not want to pay for the collecting and compilation of the information; that would still be done by the government. All they want to do is publish and distribute and reap a considerable profit from information collected at the expense of taxpayers.

In order to provide for citizen access to government information, very early in our nation's history we established the Office of the Public Printer and subsequently the depository library system to make government information available through libraries around the country. By and large that system has worked very well and researchers here at Florida State as well as citizens of this area have access to a large collection of U.S. government information in the university library. Now the GPO is considering having a private contractor intervene in this system. Under its proposal a private contractor would take over the distribution of the publications to the depository libraries at little or no cost to the government, presumably because the private contractor would then be able to develop and enhance the information and sell it commercially. One can see that it is but a short time before the private contractor would point out that it could even pay the government a return if it did not have to provide free copies to the depository libraries. The GPO is preparing a pilot test to determine the feasibility of such a system.

Public Printer Ralph Kennickell has apparently done a dramatic turnabout since he made this statement to Rep. George Brown last summer:"It troubles me that some people want to privatize everything. Now when you deal with government information you've got to either take it all or leave it all alone. And I know that there are a lot of people who would love to have the information dissemination of the *Congressional Record.* They would love to have the information dissemination of the *Federal Register,* and the *Commerce Bulletin.* But they're not willing to disseminate the books on ticks; they're not willing to disseminate the books on how to take care of your babies, all the other child-care books and products . . . if you have to make a buck on something, you are not going to carry the dogs. . . . And GPO does not, or the government, I should say, does not copyright its information. For example, if I sell the franchise handbook from Commerce, there is nothing to prevent the private sector from buying a copy, cutting off the cover and reprinting this product on its own, putting a new cover on it, and selling it for any price--which has happened to that publication. But I submit to you, sir, that I think Government information is a take it all or leave it all proposition, and you can't go in there and pick this thing apart. It's just too important." The American library community couldn't agree more with Mr. Kennickell.

Contracting Out Library and Information Services

One of the more subtle, yet in the long run potentially more serious, assaults on our need to know relates to the issue of contracting out federal library and information services. Under the provisions of OMB policy Circular A-76, federal agencies must conduct studies of a long list of services to determine if those services can be carried out more economically by a private contractor than by government employees. One of the services so identified is library and information services. Once a service is identified for contracting out, proposals are invited from private contractors as well as from the government employees currently providing the service. In effect these government employees are submitting a bid to retain the jobs they may have been doing for some time. The agency then accepts the lowest proposal it receives. Many people are bothered by the notion of private contractors operating government information services no matter what controls are retained by the agency, but there are many other problems with contracting out.

7

The ludicrousness of the situation is perhaps no where more clearly seen than in the proposal of the National Oceanic and Atmospheric Administration's (NOAA) proposal to contract out its central library services. This is the same NOAA, you will recall, that the Reagan administration at one point wanted to sell to private interests. In the NOAA case the decision to contract out the library was based on flawed proposals in that the private contractors bid on a different scope of work than did the government employees. Furthermore, the private contractors' bid assumed that the contractors' cost would decline in future years because volunteers would come forward to operate the library. The proposal does not address the inevitable questions of where do these volunteers come from, what are their qualifications, and who controls them? The most frightening aspect of the entire matter is that the contractor is owned by a foreign firm, so that we will have the information service of a U.S. government agency being operated by a foreign owned corporation and staffed with volunteers.

Interestingly enough, the FBI apparently does not share the OMB's enthusiasm for having U.S. information, even unclassified information, in the hands of foreign nationals. At the same time as the NOAA situation was occurring the FBI was sending its agencies into libraries asking the staffs of those libraries to spy on the information usage of foreign nationals who might be using materials for intelligence gathering purposes. Apparently the FBI is concerned about foreign nationals obtaining information in U.S. libraries even if the OMB is not.

Control of Ideas by Private Groups

You should not leave with the impression that only the federal government, in the name of economy, is curtailing or giving away to the private sector most of its information, thus endangering the need to know. Even if we could cure the federal problem, there is a growing number of private groups that seek to control or narrow our need to know. A detailed examination of current censorship efforts in our country is not appropriate for this conference, but we need to remember that such efforts are growing.

Censorship Efforts in Schools and Libraries

Almost daily we read about new efforts of various groups of people to have books removed from public and school libraries because they find the contents of those books offensive to their ideas or to their religion. In recent years those efforts at censorship have centered more and more on public schools and on their libraries. We are in the process of forging a new base of case law based on a long series of court decisions that balance rights and duties of school boards to control the local schools against the First Amendment rights of students and parents. The issues are thorny and not easily sorted out, but the ALA and other groups seems to have the courts moving toward the view that while school boards do indeed have wide latitude in curriculum matters they cannot exclude material and ideas from the schools simply because they or other groups personally find them unattractive. This legal principle is far from established, and even if it were the cases would not stop. I believe that most censorship efforts in this country are not intellectual but emotional. People who seek to remove books are not doing so because of the ideas; in many cases they have never even seen or read the materials. They wish to censor because of frustration. People are saying, in effect, I cannot do anything about nuclear weapons or Star Wars, I cannot affect the economy. AIDS scares me today for myself and my children, but I cannot really do anything about it. I cannot reduce the national debt, but I can do something about the books my kid brings home from the school or public library and I am going to do it.

Secular Humanism

The religious right has found a new straw man enemy called *secular humanism* and is rallying its forces in great fervor to resist this enemy. It makes a great enemy because it is not clearly defined and is assumed to be pervasive, so that almost anything can be attacked as secular humanism. Secular humanism is the greatest bugaboo since witches and communists in government have gone out of style. Basically secular humanism is anything that suggests that people do have free will and can control their own lives and must take responsibility for their decisions. The battles are growing, and the territory includes textbooks, teaching content and methods, library books, and indeed the lifestyles of teachers, librarians, and public officials of all kinds. Secular humanism is a broad brush that can smear everything from the United Nations to the local Planned Parenthood chapter. The struggle over secular humanism will be with us for some time to come and will have a very direct impact upon our need to know as various groups label various kinds of knowledge and attempt to control our right to have access.

Conclusion

In his long poem *The Rock*, T. S. Eliot asks the wonderful question, "Where is the knowledge, we have lost in information?" I believe that question to be one of the essential questions of our time. How can we extract knowledge, which we may also define as truth, certainty, or security, from the mass of information all about us. No concerned person in America lacks information about the Iran-Contra mess, for example, but we all still lack knowledge. The inability to organize information into meaningful and useful patterns frustrates our need to know enormously. A recent article in the *Wall Street Journal* details the fact that we have been able to analyze only about 10 percent of the information retrieved from our many space ventures because we lack the software and the personnel. A sole librarian is working to develop an electronic catalog of the tapes that better describes their contents so that scientists can find what they want. Thus far only 1 percent of the tapes has been cataloged and most of the tapes collected in the last two decades may never be listed. To get a picture of the problem, consider that the 1974 Hawkeye satellite transmitted 86.4 million bits of information per day for four years. In 1979 the Hubbel Space Telescope transmitted 4.32 billion bits per day and will do so for fifteen years. The proposed space station to be launched between 1994 and 1997 will transmit ten trillion bits per day for up to thirty years.

In case you think that this problem simply deals with a mass of technical unorganized data of little value, the *Journal* article points out that the hole in the earth's ozone layer, which scientists believe can have serious long-term effects in heating up our atmosphere and significantly raising water levels by the premature melting of glaciers, could have been discovered and dealt with a decade earlier by analyzing the data obtained by the Nimbus satellite. This information is stored around the country in what scientists call tape landfills. Nasa has 73,000 tapes stacked in one records center and hundreds of thousands more in labs across the country and is not even sure how many it has.

As a people we do not lack for information. In fact we have reached the point that in many cases, if there is not guided access to information, then the information is in effect denied, because users simply cannot obtain it on their own or even learn of its existence. When NOAA permits its libraries to be staffed by volunteers, it is not simply reducing its budget, it is also denying access to information. When the local county commission decides, as it did this week to increase hours at the public library without increasing the staff available it is not simply getting more for its money, but is frustrating our need to know, because without guided access to a collection we cannot know. It is somewhat ironic that the U.S. Supreme Court has held that if we put people in jail we must either provide them with access to legal counsel or to a law library in order to enable them to get the information they need to establish their innocence. How unfortunate that we do not have the same concern for those citizens who are not incarcerated. Whether we like it or not, whether we wish it or not, we are being driven by the forces outlined above to a society in which our need to know is being held hostage to our ability to pay. Access to information, because of the sheer bulk of it, must be paid for because someone must be paid to organize it for us. We must decide how we wish to have those payments made. In the past we have made them partly as individuals when we purchased books, magazines, and newspapers that we wished to own and partly through public enterprises when the government published information or when libraries acquired information and organized it to be available for our use. Now we are being forced to re-examine those decisions and the kind of choices we make will determine what happens to our need to know.

If we opt to call on the private sector to be our information collector, organizer, and deliverer, we are making a choice that will be very efficient but also very discriminating. Those who can pay the most will get the most and the information that does not attract a lot of payers will not be collected or organized. If we call on the public sector we may indeed sacrifice a measure of cost efficiency but we gain the value that the least important citizen will have access equal to the most important. As a people, I think, we basically believe that a person's health care should not be dependent upon their ability to pay for it. We have not yet reached that goal but we do hold it and work toward it. We do not seem to have developed the same national consensus about our knowledge health. Yet it is clear that decisions that can significantly affect our knowledge health are being made every day. I hope that in this conference and in the near future we can begin to hammer out a consensus policy that will keep our need to know in a healthy state.

PART 1
The Government's Philosophy and Practice

OMB Perspective on Electronic Collection and Dissemination of Information

J. TIMOTHY SPREHE

Senior Policy Analyst
Office of Management and Budget
Washington, D.C.

The Office of Management and Budget (OMB) issued OMB Circular No. A-130, Management of Federal Information Resources, in December 1985.[1] The arrival of this document setting forth general guidelines as to how federal agencies should manage information and information technology had been long awaited and repeatedly called for.[2] Whatever its merits--and they continue to be debated--the appearance of Circular No. A-130 has at least satisfied the congressional and public demand for a comprehensive federal information policy.

Indeed, Congress has paid the circular the compliment of writing into law a requirement for its continued existence. The original Paperwork Reduction Act stipulated "general information policy" functions for the OMB, which were to include developing and implementing uniform and consistent information resources management policies and overseeing the development of information management principles, standards, and guidelines and promoting their use.[3]

When the act was reauthorized in 1986, among the amendments enacted was a requirement that the OMB "maintain a comprehensive set of information resources management policies."[4] The legislative history explained that: language in S. 2433, 98th Congress, would have required the OMB to "develop and issue" a comprehensive set of such policies. In

December 1985, OMB issued Circular No. A-130, which provides a general policy framework for management of federal information resources. Therefore, this paragraph requires OMB to maintain this policy.[5]

While this statement does not necessarily endorse the contents of Circular No. A-130, it does appear to acknowledge that, in the eyes of Congress, the Circular satisfies the act's requirement for issuance of general information policy. If the OMB had not issued Circular No. A-130, Congress presumably would have taken some steps to enforce the requirement in law.

Information Collection and Dissemination in the Paperwork Reduction Act

The law popularly called the Paperwork Reduction Act (Title 44, Chapter 35 of the *United States Code*)in fact has many purposes beyond reducing the burden the government imposes on the public through information collection. To be sure, the act does have as its very first purpose "to minimize the federal paperwork burden for individuals, small businesses, state and local government, and other persons."[6] This purpose is carried out in part by the information collection request and other paperwork control functions assigned to the Director of the Office of Management and Budget (OMB). But the act assigns five other functions to the OMB, and perhaps most notably, the title of the act, *as codified*, is Coordination of Federal Information Policy.[7]

The OMB's control over information collections arises from the Paperwork Reduction Act's explicit requirement that the OMB review and approve individual information collection requests proposed by federal agencies. The OMB must determine, on a case by case basis, whether an information collection has practical utility and is necessary for the proper performance of agency functions. The OMB has the authority under the act to disapprove individual information collections.[8]

By contrast, the original Paperwork Reduction Act contained but a handful of occurrences of the word "dissemination." In section 3504 on the authority and functions of the OMB, dissemination occurs only with respect to statistical policy and coordination and with respect to ADP functions, not with respect to general information policy functions.

In drafting Circular No. A-130, the OMB believed it could not issue comprehensive policy on information resources management without including policy on information dissemination. The concept of information resources management, although not specifically defined in the original Paperwork Reduction Act, clearly encompassed the life cycle of information from creation through dissemination to final disposition. A policy intended to govern agency behavior with respect to the information life cycle would be notably incomplete if it failed to treat dissemination, a major step in the cycle.

In the 1986 amendments to the act, Congress implicitly supported the OMB's reasoning about dissemination. The amendments introduced a generous sprinkling of the word "dissemination" throughout the text of the act. The purpose of the act is expanded to include the word, and the authority and functions of the OMB are similarly changed. Dissemination is said to be a key information management area not specified in the original act but increasingly important in recent years.[9] The report of the Senate Committee on Governmental Affairs states: "Management of the federal government's information resources includes all stages of information management and all types of information technology. . . . Such management also includes planning and organizing for the efficient and coordinated collection, use and dissemination of information, and properly training employees to carry out such tasks."[10]

Even though the act now uses the word dissemination frequently, it still contains no detailed authorities, functions, or tasks with respect to dissemination. Authorities and functions for information collection were sufficiently specific that the OMB issued a regulation on Controlling Paperwork Burden on the Public[11] rather than a circular; a regulation is stronger than a circular, having the force of law. This specificity does not exist in the law for dissemination. The act, for example, does not give the OMB the authority to disapprove agency information dissemination products or services.[12] It is therefore the broader authorities under the act that provide the basis for the information dissemination policy found in Circular A-130.

Policy Issues in Electronic Collection

Dozens of federal agencies are currently exploring or actively conducting electronic information collection programs. Of particular interest to the agencies is the potential of electronic collection by itself; that is, the collection by electronic media of information that will not be electronically disseminated (or will be electronically disseminated only in aggregated form).

- The Internal Revenue Service (IRS) is broadening its experimental program for electronic filing of individual income tax returns. Qualified return preparers electronically transmitted individual income tax returns for tax year 1986 to the IRS on behalf of clients. Electronic returns were filed from seven metropolitan areas (up from three in the previous year), and taxpayers filing in three of these areas were able to elect to have their refunds directly deposited in their bank accounts. The principal advantages of electronic filing are: (1) taxpayers will receive refunds two or three weeks faster than if their returns had been filed on paper; (2) return preparers will be able to serve clients more efficiently; (3) the cost to IRS of processing, storing, and retrieving these returns will be substantially reduced; and (4) taxpayers participating in direct deposit will obtain their refunds quickly and more conveniently.

- Since 1984, the Social Security Administration (SSA) has been encouraging employers to report wage data (W-2 forms) electronically. SSA expected to receive over 60 million W-2s electronically in 1986 and 105 million by 1989. All employers with more than 500 employees must report electronically after 1 January 1987; after 1 January 1988, all employers with more than 250 employees are so covered. The primary benefits from electronic collection have been a reduction in the duplication of effort entailed in paper transactions, receipt of better service from SSA, and enhanced efficiencies in information handling. SSA has particularly benefited from more timely posting of earnings as well as reductions in manual activities, errors, and backlogs of paper, tape, and diskette handling. SSA expected a paperwork burden reduction of over 1.3 million hours due to this initiative in 1986 and an additional 1.9 million hour reduction in 1987.

- The Department of Education is testing the feasibility of major electronic collection projects involving student aid programs: the Gateway and Pell Grant Pilot projects. The Gateway project would provide for electronic processing of the Fiscal Operations Report and Application to Participate, a major reporting requirement for campus-based programs. Respondents may transmit online or via diskette. The Pell Grant Pilot project encompasses the electronic transfer of information associated with the Student Aid Report. The total size of the data collections affected by these activities exceeds 300,000 burden hours annually.

- The Department of Labor, Pension Benefit Guaranty Corporation, Internal Revenue Service, and Social Security Administration are jointly studying, under OMB chairmanship, automation of Form 5500, an annual report from every administrator of a pension plan as required by the Employee Retirement Income Security Act (ERISA). Currently, plan sponsors of over 900,000 employee benefit plans file paper copies of their annual reports with the IRS. Due to delays in verification, user agencies must wait almost a year for access to the data, and this reduces the ability of the agencies to undertake necessary research and enforcement activities. The interagency group is examining alternative filing and processing procedures to yield not only a paperwork burden savings for the benefit plan community but also more effective use of the information collected. Form 5500 currently imposes 3.2 million burden hours each year; through automation the agencies expect to reduce the burden by almost 500,000 hours over the next several years.

- The Energy Information Administration, Department of Energy, has successfully implemented a microcomputer-based data collection for reporting radioactive waste from civilian nuclear reactors. EIA provides respondents with microcomputer software and data diskettes. Respondents verify and update the previous year's data and enter current year data on the data diskettes. EIA analysts review, edit, and verify the received data on microcomputers, and then transfer clean data files to the EIA mainframe computer for storage, aggregation, and distribution. EIA finds that the system reduces reporting errors and greatly speeds the reporting cycle.

- The U.S. Customs Service has initiated the Customs Automated Commercial System (ACS) to link electronically import-export brokers and shippers with customs' computer system, and thereby reduce the paperwork flow between customs and the public. ACS enables brokers to transmit directly to customs the information about their client's cargo necessary to assess the proper tariff. The system provides interactive communications between customs and the affected public. Customs is able to release the cargo more quickly, determine the proper tariff, and obtain payment from the broker periodically instead of obtaining payment at the time the tariff is computed for each individual shipment. Customs anticipates a reduction of approximately one million burden hours for the affected public by late 1988 as a result of ACS.

The focus in the foregoing examples is on efficiencies accruing to the agencies receiving the information and to the public providing the information. The agencies realize cost avoidances from reductions in error rates; decreased costs in information collection or capture; and increased timeliness in processing and publishing (either internally or externally) the information. The responding publics report some reductions in the burden and cost of providing information, and other benefits such as greater convenience, faster receipt of government response, and the ability to do business more efficiently with the government. So long as both the agencies and the public are receiving these benefits and the costs of conversion to electronic collection are modest, electronic collection will continue to grow rapidly.

In August 1987, the OMB published proposed policy guidance on electronic collection of information,[13] and in November made available a summary of comments received from the public.[14] (See the appendix to this essay for a summary of the proposed policy and of the public's response.)

Policy Issues in Electronic Dissemination of Information

With the exception of the smallest independent agencies, almost every federal agency now electronically disseminates information products to the public: on magnetic tape, floppy disk, and CD ROM; via electronic bulletin boards and via online information services.[15] The Bureau of the Census, for example, has been selling magnetic tapes of its data products to the public for twenty years and at present offers about 750 titles on electronic media. The National Library of Medicine began making its holdings available electronically in 1970 and today offers online services to thirty MEDLARS databases. The National Archives and Records Administration, as the nation's repository for federal records, stores and distributes magnetic tapes from more than fifty agencies. The Commerce Department's National Technical Information Service receives electronic products from other agencies and currently sells about 2,600 titles to the public.

While electronic dissemination has been common for several decades, contemporary concern revolves around programs for "electronic filing." As a popular catchall phrase the term is misleading because most people associate filing with recordkeeping rather than information collection and because it fails to convey the key feature that electronic filing projects integrate collection and dissemination within a single system.

The best known electronic filing project is doubtless the Securities and Exchange Commission's (SEC's) EDGAR (for Electronic Data Gathering, Analysis, and Retrieval). EDGAR is designed to automate filing, processing, and dissemination of 7 million pages of filings. This system should improve the effectiveness of SEC processing of filings, and ensure rapid, timely disclosure of information to investors and the financial community.

Almost equally well known is the Patent and Trademark Office's automation plan, designed to automate, among other things, search files holding over 27 million patent related documents. Similarly, the Federal Maritime Commission is studying the feasibility of electronic filing of maritime tariffs, the Department of Transportation is investigating electronic filing of international air cargo and passenger tariffs, and the Interstate Commerce Commission plans to permit electronic filing of tariffs.

Because of increased federal agency activity in electronic collection and dissemination, coupled with congressional and public interest, the OMB committed to revising Circular No. A-130 by the end of fiscal year 1988 so as to provide guidance on electronic collection and dissemination of information. While this work is still in progress, a beginning has been made on electronic collection policy and on the likely issue areas for electronic dissemination policy. These areas are as follows.

- *Incorporation of OMB Circular No. A-3; Agency Inventories.* Title 44, *United States Code*, Section 1108, dating from 1922, requires agencies to seek OMB approval before using funds to print periodicals. The OMB currently implements section 1108 through OMB Circular No. A-3, Government Publications, revised 2 May 1985. The circular requires agencies to seek OMB approval for periodicals; to submit an annual statistical report on agency publications; and to maintain an OMB-approved publications control plan.

The OMB plans to incorporate Circular No. A-3 into Circular No. A-130, to require agencies to maintain in electronic form an up-to-date inventory of their information dissemination products, and to include in the inventory electronic as well as printed products.

- *Adequate Notice.* Circular No. A-130 required agencies to "disseminate significant new, or terminate significant existing, information products and services only after providing adequate notice to the public." (Section 8a [10]) Appendix IV to the circular advised that agencies should themselves determine the meaning of "significant" and suggested that agencies develop procedures for adequate notice.

The OMB has received few indications that agencies have in fact developed such procedures, and has heard numerous complaints of violations of the policy, particularly with regard to initiating electronic dissemination products. The revision to Circular No. A-130 will provide more specific guidance on the issue of adequate notice.

- *Other General Guidance.* Other issues to be considered include whether agencies should sell their databases or only services derived from databases; whether agencies should wholesale or retail their information products; whether and to what extent agencies are obliged to survey the marketplace before offering new information products; and what are appropriate user charges for electronic information products.

The OMB plans next to publish proposed policy guidance on electronic dissemination of information, addressing some of the issue areas suggested above. After receiving comments, the OMB will combine the policy for electronic collection and dissemination, and issue a single integrated appendix to OMB Circular A-130 dealing with both subjects.

APPENDIX

Description of August 1987 Notice on Electronic Collection of Information

The proposed guidance stated first that agencies should certify for each information collection that they have considered use of electronic collection techniques.[16]

Second, the proposed policy enumerated conditions said to be favorable to electronic collection. The conditions were:

1. The agency routinely converts the information collected to electronic format.

2. A substantial proportion of respondents are known to possess the necessary information technology and to maintain the information in electronic form.

3. Conversion to electronic reporting, if mandatory, will not impose substantial costs or other adverse effects on respondents, especially small business entities.

4. The information collection seeks a relatively large volume of data and/or reaches a large number of respondents.

5. The information collection is relatively frequent; that is, annually or more frequently.

6. The content and format of the information sought by the information collection does not change significantly over several years.

When these conditions are met, the proposed policy stated that agencies should conduct benefit-cost analyses and, where results so indicate, actively pursue design and development of electronic collection.

Third, the proposed policy suggested some criteria for design and development of electronic collection systems. The systems should take due account of the Privacy Act and Freedom of Information Act. They should avoid attempting to have the private sector finance governmental functions within the systems, as appeared to be the case in earlier versions of the EDGAR project. Essentially, SEC believed that its contractor's sale of the EDGAR database should generate sufficient revenues to finance the contract; hence SEC originally planned to put no appropriated funds into the contract. Congress disagreed with this strategy and insisted on the view that governmental functions should be paid for with appropriated funds.

Where electronic reporting is mandatory, waiver procedures should be available for those who will incur unreasonable costs, permitting them to report on paper. On the one hand, small businesses should not be financially burdened with having to acquire the information technology necessary to report electronically. On the other hand, where there is substantial value to the public in having all respondents' data in the database, and where respondents could "game the system" by the medium of reporting they choose, it is desirable to build in strong incentives for using electronic reporting and for minimizing waivers.

Where collection and dissemination are to be combined in the same overall system, the two functions (as well as records management) should be integrated into a single system design. In too many cases, the failure to integrate the two functions results in systems with serious deficiencies in public access and dissemination.

The OMB received a total of thirty-five comments on the notice. Twenty-seven comments came from federal agencies; one from Congress; the remainder were trade associations, firms, and individual members of the public.

The distribution of comments indicates that electronic collection, taken by itself, is primarily of interest to federal agencies, rather than the general public. The great majority of commenters expressed general support for the policy guidance. No one voiced general opposition to the policy. Some of the issues raised by the commenters are discussed below.

Is Electronic Collection Less Burdensome? One commenter noted that the proposed policy tends to assume electronic collection will be less burdensome to the public than conventional collection. The commenter believed this a questionable assumption, pointing out the possibility that in some cases the response burden for electronic collection could actually be greater, and that in any event a change in information collection practices should be accompanied by a new estimate of response burden.

The amount of time it takes the public to fill out government-sponsored forms is the principal yardstick the Paperwork Reduction Act uses for assessing the burden of government information collections. It may well be that responding electronically could take more time in certain cases, and yet the public might greatly prefer this medium because of other benefits such as faster tax refund checks, which are not possible with conventional paper response. Indeed it is arguably more efficient in this example for the public to spend more time on answering the forms electronically in order to gain the return of cash in hand earlier; in effect one exchanges capital efficiencies for labor inefficiencies.

Benefit-Cost Analysis. Many commenters focused on the language concerning benefit-cost analysis. Federal agency comments ranged from a recommendation that the OMB develop guidance on the benefit-cost analysis to serious objections to a requirement for such analysis. In the latter category, several agencies believed a benefit-cost requirement could be costly and time consuming to the agency. One agency stated that candidate information collections could be chosen through sound programmatic and financial management practices rather than through a benefit-cost requirement. A private sector commenter urged that agencies especially examine the benefit-costs for small businesses, especially where small businesses receive no benefits from electronic collection.

Advisability of Waivers. Several members of the public commented to the effect that waiver procedures, permitting respondents to report by conventional methods, should be kept to a minimum so that government databases remain comprehensive. Where waivers permit paper responses, these commenters believed the agencies should convert the responses to electronic media.

Notes

This presentation is based on a paper prepared for *Government Information Quarterly*, Summer 1988.

1. Office of Management and Budget, "Management of Federal Information Resources: Final Publication of OMB Circular No. A-130," *Federal Register* 50 (24 December 1985): 52730-52751. Hereafter, OMB Circular No. A-130.

2. J. Timothy Sprehe, "OMB Circular No. A-130, the Management of Federal Information Resources: Its Origins and Impact," *Government Information Quarterly* 4 (1987): 189-96.

3. Title 44, *United States Code*, Section 3504 (b)(1).

4. Paperwork Reduction Act, as amended, Title 44 *United States Code*, Section 3505(5).

5. Senate Committee on Governmental Affairs, Report on Federal Management Reorganization and Cost Control Act of 1986, 99th Congress, Report No. 99-347, 31 July 1986, 55. Hereafter, Senate Committee on Governmental Affairs.

6. Title 44, *United States Code*, Section 3501.

7. The five other functions to be performed by the OMB under the act are: (1) to develop and implement general information policies, principles, standards, and guidelines; (2) to provide policy and coordination for federal statistical activities; (3) to oversee federal records management; (4) to provide policy guidance on privacy and security of records; and (5) to

provide policy and coordination on federal automatic data processing and telecommunications. Title 44, *United States Code*, Section 3504.

8. See Title 5, *Code of Federal Regulations*, Part 1320. Hereafter, 5 CFR 1320. The OMB also has the authority under the act to delegate its case-by-case approval authority to the agencies. See 44 U.S.C. 3507(e).

9. Senate Committee on Governmental Affairs, 54.

10. Ibid., 53.

11. 5 CFR 1320.

12. OMB Circular No. A-130, Government Publications, implements Title 44, *United States Code*, Section 1108, which requires agencies to seek OMB approval before using funds for printing of periodicals.

13. Office of Management and Budget, "Notice of Policy Guidance on Electronic Collection of Information," *Federal Register* 52 (7 August 1987): 29454-29457.

14. Office of Information and Regulatory Affairs, Office of Management and Budget, "Summary of Comments on Office of Management and Budget's Notice of Policy Guidance on Electronic Collection of Information," Washington, D.C., 17 November 1987.

15. For a directory of most of the electronic products available from federal agencies, see Sharon Zarozny, ed., *The Federal Database Finder*, 2d ed. (Chevy Chase, Md.: Information USA, Inc., 1987).

16. The appendix was adapted from the OMB's "Notice of Policy Guidance on Electronic Collection of Information," 29454-29457, and from the "Summary of Comments" on the notice.

The Congressional Role

BERNADINE ABBOTT HODUSKI

Professional Staff Member for Library and Distribution Services
U.S. Congress Joint Committee on Printing
Washington, D.C.

In the foreword to the bicentennial edition of the Constitution of the United States, former Representative Peter Rodino sums up the philosophy under which all of us in the federal government work: "The body of the Constitution sets up a system of internal checks and balances which, at times, may appear to be unduly cumbersome, but which succeeds in preventing any part of the government from having absolute power. Under our Constitution, it is not only the people who are made to adhere to principles of justice and the rule of law, but government itself. The citizen thus has the power--and indeed the obligation--to vigilantly safeguard the guarantees and freedoms contained in the Constitution."

The policies and framework under which information is collected, managed, and shared is constantly being formulated because the three branches of government as well as the people are involved in its formulation. It is only natural that the executive, legislative and judicial branches will compete for control over the basic policies affecting information, since all three branches recognize the power and the need for information. All three collect and publish information in one way or another. Each branch of government wants the information held by the other and through the years they have compromised on ways of sharing that information. Each branch also wants to control its own means of publication.

In the last few years we have seen many examples of the struggle between the executive and legislative branches about what and how much

27

information will be shared, not only within government but with the people. The most dramatic recent struggle is that concerning information about our government's relationship with Iran. The Congress considered the information it gathered of such interest to the public that it ignored its own traditional adherence to muted colors and conservative paper in order to publish its report with a colorful slick cover.

It is difficult at times for the other branches of government and the public to determine who within Congress is making policy, because so many committees play a role in establishing and debating policy. Sometimes the Congress will even pass conflicting laws that later have to be looked at by the judicial branch and returned to Congress for reconciliation. But one thing you should be aware of, Congress is very jealous of its power to determine information policies and will not give that up lightly. For example, in 1979, the Joint Committee on Printing and its parent legislative committees, (House Administration and Senate Rules) wrote a bill to abolish the Government Printing Office as well as the Joint Committee on Printing and in their place establish an independent agency, whose board would be composed of representatives from all three branches of government as well as the public. The House Government Operations Committee objected to the agency being outside the legislative branch and we rewrote the bill to accommodate their concerns.

Every legislative committee at some time has played a role in establishing information policy. It varies from an authorizing committee writing a bill that directs an agency to collect and publish certain information to the appropriations committees including in the appropriations bills limitations on the number of copies that can be printed of certain publications. A recent example is the Public Law 100-202, the Continuing Appropriations Act for Fiscal Year 1988, which prohibits the use of funds by executive branch departments and agencies "for the procurement from commercial sources of any printing related to the production of government publications (including forms), unless such procurement is by or through the Government Printing Office."[1]

The Congress traditionally has supported both the production and the access to information of all kinds, not just government information. In the eighteenth and nineteenth centuries, the Congress was the publisher of most government publications and most of the copies printed for all three branches of government and the public came out of the legislative branch's appropriations. Congress distributed information ranging from the *Agriculture Yearbook to Infant Care*. All you have to do is look at the *United States Congressional Serial Set* over the years and you will see everything from the reports of the Lewis and Clark expeditions to the foreign relations of the United States. During and after the Second World War, government publishing became so prolific that the Congress was no longer willing to pay for most of the publishing from its own budget. But it was not until the 1970s that Congress systematically began directing the executive and judicial branches to pay for their own copies of such publications as the *United States Code* and the *Federal Register*. All of those major publications used to be supported from a general fund appropriated to the legislative branch.

Congress has always strongly supported research, collection, and dissemination of information generated from many sources. The Congress itself is both a major publisher and consumer of information. The Congress has through the years supported the exchange of information with state and local governments, the public, and foreign governments. From the very beginning the three branches have used libraries as a vehicle for sharing information with each other and the public. The depository library program includes libraries from all three branches of government, as well as libraries outside the government, and is a practical, economical way to share information. The depository library program is only effective if all three branches cooperate and make their information available for sharing.

Congress has in the 100th Congress and will in the 101st Congress make important policy decisions in the area of government information. Because Congress knows that they do not have all the information they need to make decisions, they established a number of support agencies to assist them in gathering and analyzing the needed information. Those support agencies include the Office of Technology Assessment (OTA), the Congressional Budget Office (CBO), the General Accounting Office (GAO), and the Congressional Research Service (CRS) (Library of Congress).

Most recently, the Joint Committee on Printing, the House Committee on Government Operations, and a number of other committees asked the OTA to look at new technologies in relation to the dissemination of government information. The OTA issued its draft report entitled "Informing the Nation: The Future of Federal Electronic Printing, Publishing, and Dissemination" on 3 May 1988 before publishing the final version sometime in the fall of 1988.

The General Accounting Office, at the request of the Joint Committee on Printing, conducted a survey of libraries, professional organizations, and agencies, requesting information on their government information publishing and printing needs for the future. The results of the survey of federal agencies will be published in August of 1988 under the title "Information Management: Federal Agencies Needs and Practices." The results of the libraries and organizations survey will be published together under a similar title in the late fall of 1988.

The survey of the federal agencies concentrated on the following areas: agencies' use of new technologies, agencies' evaluation of the quality of GPO services, quantitative data on agency electronic databases, including electronic bulletin boards, and how much data agencies disseminate to the public in electronic form.

The GAO asked the libraries and organizations a series of questions designed to aid the Joint Committee on Printing and the GPO in determining the customers' future needs. A particular emphasis was placed on determining their interest in receiving government information in electronic format and whether they have or are planning on acquiring the needed equipment to access data in that format. Preliminary results show that 69.6 percent (thirty-two of the forty-six) of the regional depository libraries have CD ROM readers and that 38.4 percent of the selective depository libraries have CD ROM readers.

The Joint Committee on Printing, based upon advice of its advisory group, the Ad Hoc Committee on Depository Library Access to Federal Automated Data Bases, passed a resolution in April of 1987 calling for "a series of pilot projects [to] be implemented to test the feasibility and practicality of disseminating government publications to depository libraries in electronic formats."[2] As a result of this resolution, the GPO in consultation with the Joint Committee produced a plan entitled "Dissemination of Information in Electronic Format to Federal Depository Libraries: Proposed Project Descriptions" in June 1988. The Joint Committee accepted that plan on 29 June 1988 and distributed it for public comment.

The demonstration projects include CD ROM and on-line projects and will be done in cooperation with the publishing agencies. The type of data includes statistical as well as full text. The subjects range from census data to scientific and legislative material. The first project will be the distribution of the *1982 Census of Retail Trade by Zip Code* and the *1982 Census of Agriculture* on CD ROM. All 1400 depository libraries will receive a CD, floppy disk with software, documentation, and an evaluation questionnaire. All depository libraries are in this project because the Census Bureau will be a major producer of data on CD ROM. Much of the census data, such as the block maps, will be too voluminous for publication on paper or microfiche, and the only reasonable form of publication is electronic.

A number of agencies and outside groups are studying and preparing reports and recommendations in the area of government information policy. The Smithsonian Institution Working Group on Electronic Publishing released its report "Electronic Publishing for SI Research" in May 1988 and Jerry Berman of the American Civil Liberties Union is working on a paper entitled "Communications Policy and the Public's Right to Know: Democratizing Citizen Access to Electronic Public Information." The Department of Commerce has drafted a proposed administrative order on electronic information dissemination based upon the framework established by the Office of Management and Budget's Circular A-130, "Management of Federal Information Resources."

There is a lot of policy making in the works. You as librarians and publishers need to keep informed about these efforts and react to them, or the needs of your users will not be considered when the final policies are adopted and implemented.

Notes

1.   The Appropriations Committees included the same directive in the fiscal year 1989 appropriations bill.

2.   U.S. Congress, Joint Committee on Printing, committee resolution, 100th Congress, 1st session, 1987.

PART 2
The Private Sector's
Philosophy and Role

The View from the Information Industry Association

PAUL G. ZURKOWSKI

Executive Director, Information Industry Association
Washington, D.C.

This year we are celebrating the twentieth anniversary of the founding of Information Industry Association (IIA). Over the last twenty years, we in the industry have faced eleven new technologies.

1. The first is ink on paper, which was around a long time before we got started. Twenty years ago, it was the predominant way of disseminating information. It still is today.

2. With third generation computers in the mid-1960s, you began to be able to computer compose a whole page of copy within the computer. Subsequently, the industry developed the ability to switch from printing codes to search codes and you got to the tape spinning age. A database company sent its tapes to a university computing center where, through batch processing, users got access to the contents.

3. Early in the 1970s along came packet switching. Telenet and Tymnet began providing remote access to the databases linked by telephone. Packet switching allows timesharing of the telephone lines and makes access to remotely stored data comparatively inexpensive.

4.   That was followed by full text. Mead Data Central pioneered this development.

5.   That in turn was followed by videotext. Videotext came along toward the end of the 1970s and at least opened the eyes of people to simple search strategies.

6.   That was followed by optical media, which got started at about the same time as the personal computer.

7.   I think the personal computer providing intelligence at the receiving end of the dissemination system has been terribly underutilized by this industry. It has not taken off as people had expected it to.

8.   In addition to that, there was artificial intelligence and expert systems.

9.   Right now we are heavily into the voice information environment.

10.   ISDN, local area networks, satellites, FM sideband, point-to-multipoint distribution comprise the tenth technology.

11.   The eleventh is fifth generation computers, which will really make artificial intelligence lively and possible.

In the twenty years that the association has been around, the industry has had to cope and contend with, master, decide whether to use it or not, and develop competing products with these eleven technologies. It is a daunting experience to say the least.

As all of that was playing out, we in IIA created a map of the information industry (see figure 1). As you look at the map, the upper-right-hand corner includes content services covering a whole array. You will notice that libraries are in this segment as well as information-on-demand services, and databases. We have also added videotext and voice services.

Newsletters overlap into the next segment of the map, content packages, literally stand-alone packages of information. Recent additions are CD ROM and CDI publishing.

One of the most active areas in the information business is facilitation services. More activity is going on in here--more startups, more new products--than you will find in the other two previous sections.

The fourth segment is information technologies. It shows an array of technologies. We have added desktop publishing, which is both a facilitator and information technology.

The four remaining sections are integrating technologies (including modems, digital switches, and facsimile), communications technologies, communication channels (we have included the European PTTs because we have the domestic versions here as well), and finally, broadcast channels.

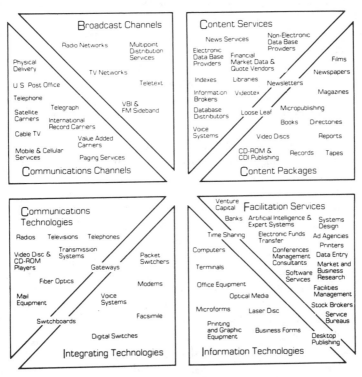

Figure 1. Map of the Information Industry

IIA provides members with services through four divisions. Voice information services is a new and emerging area. It started with us about eighteen months ago with nothing more than a committee and in that time has grown into a very active division. The voice information business is tied to the idea of the ubiquitous touch tone telephone being able to provide access to computerized databases. The voice response is digitized and prerecorded and the computer sorts out the appropriate answer depending on what the input is. For example, at Brigham Young University, students pay $10 to be able to register for classes by phone. They punch in what their major is and what course numbers they are interested in taking. The computer is programmed to tell them whether they have the necessary prerequisites, whether the course is full and what the alternatives are. It saves them from going through "gang" registration in the gymnasium or wherever.

Companies like Dun & Bradstreet have many voice information services. To get a credit rating you merely call Dun & Bradstreet. If you have the number it is a very simple procedure. By calling up and asking the appropriate questions, a prerecorded voice will have been programmed by the computer to give you the words that give you the correct information. When Dun & Bradstreet started that, a very prestigious voice was used to record all the words that needed to be used. Surprisingly, it did not work. When people heard this deep baritone voice, they hung up thinking they had reached the president of the company. All the words had to be rerecorded in a voice that was appropriate to respond to credit ratings.

The other divisions are Database and Publishing Division, Electronic Services Division, and Financial Information Services Division.

The information industry experience enlarges on what seems to be the single meaning of the word "information." It is multidimensional, and it is not clear that either a single data acquisition or a single data distribution policy can be fashioned to control it.

I view life in terms of who controls the switches of information. I think you do, too. Who is controlling your access and your ability to think thoughts by how much access you have to what has already been thought.

It is instructive to look at a period of history 500 years ago that in many ways is parallel to our own. At the time Gutenberg's press was beginning to crank out pages of the Gutenberg Bible, the people who controlled the switches of information were the monks, the guilds, and the banks. The banks controlled it for money reasons. The guilds controlled information because you had to join a guild to learn a skill as there were no "how to do it" books. The monks, dealing in the Gospel of St. John, which opens, "In the beginning was the word . . .," had convinced their contemporaries that because they were bilingual they were able to deal with the world hereafter. When you bought an indulgence you were given a 31-line indulgence form in the Greek language with a blank space for your name to be signed by the monk you bought it from.

An incident occurred in the midfifteenth century, bringing this into focus. The Turks invaded Cyprus and Pope Nicholas V authorized the massive sale of indulgences to raise money to help the Christians repel the Turks. He had heard about the printing press and sent a representative to Maintz, Germany, where Gutenberg could be found and had him "run off a few copies." They raised money selling these standard forms. The mistake they made was the forms bore the date 1454. Here was a document pretending to be eternal in nature that bore a temporal date. That led to the debunking of the myth that the monks could deal in the world hereafter in a temporal way. In fact, I once said that after Martin Luther was born in that same neck of the woods twenty years later, his bathroom was wallpapered in these forms. Somebody really believed that so I do not say that anymore.

It led, however, to Luther identifying abuses of the indulgence practice as part of the Reformation. It is not generally known that he is the first author of a printed catechism using the "new media" in an attempt to internalize the Catholic religion.

Maintz was sacked in a religious war in 1470 or thereabouts and all the disciples that had gathered at Gutenberg's feet were scattered throughout Europe, many of them going to northern Italy. By the year 1500, thousands of different volumes had been printed by the printers in northern Italy. It wasn't until the DeMedici library was formed that it was recognized that this was contributing something. Until then, literate people who could afford a copyist were hiring copyists to make beautifully illustrated books. The product coming off the printing press looked like it was coming off an early generation computer in comparison and they thought it was dehumanizing. When they got it into a library, however, it had a very significant effect.

Looking at history from the perspective of who controls the switches of information reveals many incidents. Henry VIII had a falling out with his secretary who translated the Bible for him over the translation of the New Testament. William Tindale left the King's employ and went to the continent to find a printer. Henry VIII ran him to the ground and had him burnt as a heretic.

In the United States, the first newspaper was the *Boston Newsletter*. It was published pursuant to the grant of a license, or a copyright, to make copies from the Stationers Company under the Statute of Queen Anne. When the newsletter became a seditious newspaper, the king took away its right to make copies. It was that experience that led to copyright being placed in Article I of the Constitution and not reserved for a First Amendment, second thought category. And it was truly a revolutionary development in that it vested ownership in the citizens rather than the crown for the products of the mind. It was a fundamental part of the Revolution.

One of the things that comes through to me is that libraries are just as individualistic as information companies. You each have your own constituency and you each have your own needs and you each add value and the value you add is what the community pays for when it funds a library.

Let me run through some characteristics of an information company while you try to match them up against your own experiences as a library.

Information companies develop their own products. Many of these products are very large and are beyond the capabilities of one individual to generate them. It is a team effort. The information company does get a direct copyright interest in the product that provides greater control over its use.

Information companies maintain close working relations with their customers whether its Data Resources, designing a product for a specific user based on its econometic database, or Dun & Bradstreet in the credit area, or financial information services helping marketmakers perform their jobs. They stay closely tied. They do not have a backlist mentality. They have a current demand, a current need, kind of mentality.

They develop customized products. Often the product arises from a larger database, but it serves a specific need.

Information products are oriented towards a decision-making process. That emphasizes the fact that information has value in direct proportion to what is at stake in the decision. Videotext failed in its first iteration because it delivered information that did not have value people were willing to pay for. In its second iteration, it is developing a little better approach.

Information companies are media independent. Libraries have to be media independent. If a customer is not prepared to receive information electronically, from an information company standpoint, it does not pay that company to say you are going to take that information electronically or lump it, because there is a competitor who is coming along right behind saying, we will not give it to you electronically, we will give it to you in inkprint or however you want it.

Information companies tend to place a higher value on information. They have got to. They have got to support the work force. They have to deal with production and sales problems. Who is going to do the selling job? Most information companies have underestimated how much effort it takes to sell these products because these products are unprecedented. People are trained to use the information in other ways. They have to have their habits broken and taught new ways to do it. That costs a lot of money.

Finally, information companies recognize the basic commodity is information. Once they see that, that what they have is information in manipulatable form, it changes their business outlook and their business plans.

Dun & Bradstreet, in 1965, thought of itself as a credit company. It did not issue any credit. It issued information about credit risk. When they recognized their business was information, they developed all kinds of parallel products and services.

What are the characteristics of the American economy that have given rise to this phenomenon of an information industry?

First, private ownership. Compare this to a socialist state on the other side of the Iron Curtain and there is no information industry because there is no private ownership.

There is also freedom of access to information. There is a tremendous volume of information that can be worked over and packaged and have value added to it so that there are products that can be sold.

America is data creation crazy. Develop a lot of information and there are a lot of applications for it. Once that ball starts rolling, there is a lot of demand for the services of the industry. There is widespread education. Finally, there is an entrepreneurial spirit and innovative talent.

What is the basic message this leads up to?

The information industry and libraries are in essentially the same kind of business yet I see ourselves splintering. I see positions being taken for short-term advantage. There is a richness and diversity in library resources in this country just as there is in the information industry. There are common goals and objectives. Neither of us is served when the extremists rush into positions that force us to oppose each other.

On the question of electronic publishing by GPO there is a concerted effort to exclude the information industry from participation in the discussion of how that shall be implemented. I am afraid it proceeds from the assumption that we oppose government getting into electronic publishing. We do not oppose government getting into electronic services. We want to be a partner in that. We want to participate in that process. When we have things hit us after the fact where we get a message that something has been done without us, we have no choice but to dig in our heels and say wait a minute, let us talk about that some more. That is where the situation is a little out of hand today.

What is the solution? If we go back to 100 years ago, what conditions existed? There were no child labor laws, children worked in mills sixteen hours a day, six days a week. There was no women suffrage, women were chattels, they had little place to go. There was little or no scientific publishing; America relied on German scientific publishers until after the First World War. There were no school libraries. Universities were more divinity schools than serious scientific institutions. It was a horse and buggy age. There was no communication other than by Western Union, barges, or horses. There was massive non-English speaking immigration into the U.S., with large ghettos and Eastern Europeans and Orientals clustered together without much communication. Then the Carnegie public library concept began to deal with this information poverty, this information vacuum. By the time of World War I, libraries had become known as the arsenals of democracy.

We face a different situation today. We do not face an information poverty situation. Certainly there are pockets of it. Instead, we have vast information wealth. What we need to come together on, not only you and the industry, but also the education community and the communications businesses and the hardware companies, is the need to agree on a Carnegie-like initiative that would address how we can realize the full potential of America's information wealth. We have tremendous resources. We need to develop a vision to help the U.S. leverage its world economic leadership based on its information and communication resources.

This country has a serious imbalance between a high level of information resources and a low level of information literacy. This imbalance prevents us from taking full advantage of America's lead in this last decade of the twentieth century. As this little history of where we were 100 years ago suggests, the Carnegie public library dealt with the information and knowledge vacuum. We now have a creative vacuum flowing from inadequate use of all these resources. Comparatively little energy is being applied to developing their applications. There is a creative vacuum stemming from the availability of tremendous resources going largely untapped by the vast majority of people, businesses, and government.

It is not just a question of money. American industry currently spends $40 billion a year on education and training. What is needed is a Carnegie library level initiative creating awareness of the great potential we have and focusing on the means to realize it fully--personally, professionally, corporately, nationally. Throughout this community, we need to leverage the extensive resources this country enjoys rather than quibble over turf.

We do share a lot of common objectives and goals. I would say that of the 630 member companies, 500 of them are companies that generate $1 million or less in revenues. Perhaps you can identify more readily with these smaller companies. However large or small, the information industry is made up of people who share your intense interest in the mind-expanding effect of information, the value that information delivers to the individual. This is not something anyone of us has a monopoly on. We are all working in that same vineyard. Together we can forge constructive and rapid change. Separately, we may gain a little but it will not be as much as if we come together. Together we must develop and present a sound and cost-effective means to achieve these mutual goals and I think we can easily produce the legal and policy changes necessary to implement it.

Through the Eyes of an Entrepreneur

RICHARD R. ROWE

President, The Faxon Company
Westwood, Massachusetts

I have been asked to speak on how an entrepreneur in the information services industry views the question of access to information. I will not attempt to represent others in this discussion; I am not sufficiently dispassionate for that type of an assignment. What I can talk about is the view of the Faxon Company.

At the core of our mission is the desire to provide valued services to our clients. Profit is an important by-product of that goal. First and foremost, we must satisfy our clients on an on-going basis. So when we look at the question of access, the first things we ask are: what are the needs that our clients are experiencing? What do we expect them to be experiencing in the short-run and in the long-run? And what opportunities do those needs create that we can respond to in providing services to our clients?

Underneath those questions, obviously, is the more basic one of what kind of a society do we want to have. We cannot just look at being reactive to client's needs. We try, as a company, to have the broader perspective of social goals, and we believe that effective communication within the social system is central to a democratic society and to the long-term survival of human beings on this globe. So when we think about access, we think that technology today has enabled us to generate a remarkably common vision of what we would like to have in terms of access to information.

Vision

This vision is very consistent with what John Sculley of Apple Computer has called the "knowledge navigator." On the basis of my research and in discussions with people from all around the United States, virtually everyone who works intensively with high-level information has an implicit, if not explicit, vision of the library of the future. That library is on the worker's desk.

They want a system that is personal, intelligent, and interactive. Ideally, this system is something you can talk to as distinct from having to put your hands on a keyboard.

It provides not only data in terms of numbers and words but also graphics, pictures, and voice materials in integrated fashion linked to each other. When you are reading about Winston Churchill, you can also hear his speeches on recordings. Studying Martin Luther King you can see him deliver his "I have a dream" speech in Washington, D.C. Those kinds of linking of multimedia in an integrated way--the "knowledge navigator" that we all carry around in our heads--is also networked in real time on a global basis so that whatever information we want is accessible from any point in the world instantly.

This dream, if you will, this vision of a "knowledge navigator," is something that most of us believe we will not see in our lifetime, but it implicitly drives the direction in which many of our services, particularly services that are specifically related to access, will go in the decades ahead.

In an interesting way, technology has removed all the barriers to imagining complete access to all information. So the issues I will argue today are not primarily ones of technology. In fact, technology has created issues of access that, in the past, we never dreamed that we would have to deal with. Eventually, the problem of access and the opportunity of access, depending upon your perspective, become policy issues, issues of what we would like the social system to be like. I think of them in two generic types--a more general level of policy issues, and those that are related to the financing of information.

Barriers to Access

I would like to speak to those two general categories of barriers to access this afternoon. On the more general level of policy issues there are three major needs that I think we need to clarify in order for us to have a better picture of what kind of access we want to have in the future.

First, we need help in thinking more about information. Communication, paradoxically, is a big problem in the area of information. The word *information* itself has really lost its meaning because we use it to mean so many different things. In order to have some meaningful thinking about this field, we need a better language, a taxonomy if you will, which is based on the different kinds of functions that information performs within a society. I liken it to the Eskimos and the snow. They found that one word for *snow* simply was not adequate to communicate about snow because snow was such a crucial variable in their lives. They had to have many different words for different kinds of snow--distinctions among them being in some cases life threatening. As information becomes more and more crucial to us, we find that one word will not do for *information* either.

The problem is that we have not yet really analyzed, really differentiated in our language, the different functions that information provides. We have personal kinds of information, business information, government, scientific, recreational, and military information.

There is also a distinction between what I call "hot" and "cool" information. Hot information tends to be price-insensitive; it is something that people will pay almost anything for. It tends to have a short time-frame. And it tends to be subject to privitization. Cool information tends, to be price-sensitive--I will get it only if it is cheap. It tends to be the kind of information that provides the underlying values and infrastructure of the social system. And it requires subsidy.

There is all kinds of information, and we do not have a good way of communicating the differences between them. So one plea that I would make is that some smart thinker propose a better taxonomy for us to be able to communicate in the general field.

The second policy issue has to do with the kind of access we want to provide, and for what kinds of people. One of the central groups that is critical is the poor. At this point in history--although we are increasingly moving toward universal health care and for many years we have had a universal entitlement to education for young people--we have no comparable sense as a society as to what all of our citizens in the United States should have access to in the area of information. We have a wonderful history of public libraries, free public libraries throughout the nation, but this is not supported by any explicit public policy about access to information. Given the increasing importance of information, in my opinion it is important that we have some more explicit policy as a nation, if not as a globe, with regard to what basic kinds of information every citizen should have access to.

This is not a minor, theoretical issue because in a society that is becoming more and more technologically oriented, more and more information based, we in the United States are graduating generations of citizens who are less educated than their parents. The generation in its late teens and early twenties has, on the average, less education than their parents at the very time when we need to have a work force and a citizenry that is far better educated than their parents. We are moving in the opposite direction.

Access to information for adults as well as for children will become increasingly critical as we will be forced to try to make up education in adult life, and in having an informed citizenry that did not obtain basic tools earlier in life.

A policy issue that must be addressed in any meaningful discussion of access is what we are going to do about the poor. What right do they have to basic information, and how should it be made accessible to them?

The third policy issue--the public-private role of information--relates to the ownership of information, or, as it is called in the trade, "intellectual property." This is a central concept for all of our publishing industry today. All of our copyright is a concept that has a lot of history. Technology is threatening the issue of intellectual property in many, many ways. The photocopier really began that process--and Fax machines, data processing systems, and networks threaten it even more. Scanners make it difficult to police the issue of intellectual property. It is time, it seems to me, that we readdress the issue of what we mean by intellectual property. How do we provide reasonable incentives for the private sector and for individuals to generate information so that they can get a return on it in terms of their own investments while at the same time not privatize information to the point that it essentially becomes inaccessible?

The issue of what information should be public from a social point of view is central to the issue of intellectual property. There are certain types of information--my own personal correspondence within my family, for example--that very few people would argue should be available to anyone who wants to see it. Within industry, private information is a very important principle, and that is not something that is being challenged. National security is always an issue of where that boundary is between legitimate security and attempts to cover the tracks of misbehavior within government. But the basic principles of national security, trade secrets, and patent rights in the United States are not at stake.

Privatization of Information

I perceive that what is happening today as the role of information becomes more and more central is that we are seeing more and more privatisation of information, more and more information that is being withheld from the public sector as the potential financial gain from information becomes recognized. Clearly, we want to make sure that the private sector gets a reasonable return on investment. A good argument could be made that in a society such as ours, communication process is enhanced by private enterprise, which in general, as a retailer of information, is more efficient and more effective than is government.

Still, there are certain kinds of information--weather reports on approaching hurricanes, and information on the AIDS epidemic--that should be in the public domain and that should be made available to all citizens regardless of their economic ability to purchase it or their relationship to the society that generated it.

What we need is a clearer picture of where information legitimately can be held without being made available to anyone except the owner of that information; where information should be available at a price and available to those who are willing to pay the price; and where information should be essentially subsidized by the community as a whole, society as a whole, and made universally accessible to all its citizens.

I am not proposing the kinds of information that should be in each of those categories; rather, I am saying that clarification of our information policy is increasingly important in a society that is moving toward information as one of its key economic and social ingredients.

Financial Barriers to Access

Finally, I would like to address the issue of financial barriers and what is a fair return on investment. As the value of information increases we inevitably will increase the number of sources of information through both large and small publishing enterprises. As we experience on a national and global basis more and more users of information, it is inevitable that the cost of information, particularly information that is perceived as having high value, will rise very rapidly.

Historically, we are in the habit of making decisions in the absence of information. We assume almost instinctively that most of our decisions will have to be made with very little background data or hard information. We decide on the basis of our instincts or feelings, even when pertinent information might exist but is not available. As technology makes information more and more accessible, we will see a ground swell of demand for that information as people realize they can make more informed decisions than they have in the past. So it is not just that more information exists, but that the rate of use and demand for that information will escalate sharply in the years ahead.

The Library of the Future

Historically, libraries have focused on the development of their collections, attempting to meet the needs of their users. Publishers and writers have collaborated with libraries in developing a healthy, supply-driven system in which a good library is a big library. In other words, the criterion of effectiveness has more to do with how much there is in the library than with how much of it is used.

The market is evolving, and I sense a change in librarians' attitudes-- away from collection development and toward access. There is simply too much information out there for any one organization or institution to collect it all. The price of information is going to increase, and the cost of storing that information is often far greater than the cost of buying it. Libraries will inevitably become more and more selective about what they purchase and will become increasingly adept at acquiring information, especially low-demand types of information, that their users want, even if it is not in the library. Technology will assist librarians in that process.

Libraries have to decide how they will treat this shift from a focus on collection to a focus on access. How much will libraries want to get into providing really "hot," timely information, such as stock and bond price fluctuations, that is needed instantly? That is not what they have been comfortable with in the past. The question is, what will they want to do about this in the future? Libraries will have to be much more explicit about the rules under which access will be available to different kinds of people in our society and about the way in which the cost of information, which will escalate dramatically in the years ahead, will be met.

What Is to Be Done

The National Commission on Libraries and Information Sciences, along with comparable groups from the United Kingdom and Canada, have been meeting over the last few years to discuss some general policy areas related to information. Last year, they produced a report called the Glenerin Declaration. The report had three recommendations concerning information policy that I would like to endorse as actions that should be taken over the next decade to prepare for the twenty first century.

First, there needs to be increased public debate on the issue of a "bill of basic information rights" for all citizens. What should be the fundamental entitlement of access to information for all citizens, what information should be included, and how will that entitlement be funded?

Second, there should be a reexamination of the concept of intellectual property and the conditions under which information can be privatized. This auxiliary examination must address the issue of copyright. If, on the one hand, there is no private ownership of intellectual property, there is no incentive to produce it, especially in the scientific, technical, and medical fields. On the other hand, if this type of material is privatized, then we lose the long-term benefits to our society that come from having it generated and dispensed.

Finally, we need to have, on a regular basis, a national information resource audit so that we will have some sense of what information is available and to whom, what sectors of information are growing, and what sectors are becoming less accessible. This audit would give us a picture of how information is evolving in our society. We have these kinds of reports on a regular basis about the role of money, education, and technology in our society. It is now clear that a national report on the evolution of information services and resources is necessary so that we can make informed decisions about information policy.

A Librarian's Perspective

ROBERT M. HAYES

Dean, Graduate School of Library and Information Science
University of California
Los Angeles, California

With all due respect to the assigned title for my talk, it would be presumptuous for me to pretend to speak for the profession. At best, I will be able to present my own perspective and to hope that, in doing so, I do adequate justice to more generally held professional views. At the outset, though, I face fundamental problems in definition: What is the "private sector?" What is the "profession?" I need to take at least a few minutes to discuss those definitions.

Definition of the "Private Sector"

First, what is the "private sector?" This indeed was a question that plagued the discussions during the deliberations of the Public Sector/Private Sector Task Force that I chaired some six years ago. Is the distinction between activities of government and those outside of government? Is it between those that are based on market forces and those based on political choices? Is it between those that pay taxes and those that do not?

Are the professional societies part of the private sector? The nonprofit corporations? The libraries within publicly supported universities or even those within private universities? The university presses? Information centers within all kinds of libraries? Indeed, are special libraries within companies part of the private sector, as the term is used for this session of the conference?

For the purposes of this talk, so as to provide some degree of focus for my comments, I will take the scope of the term *private sector* as follows: The private sector covers those nongovernmental organizations, or identifiable components of organizations, and individuals whose primary financial support comes from sale of products and services embodying information content.

In that definition, I am deliberately excluding the manufacturers of information hardware by focusing attention on information content, but I am including producers of software; that may be an artificial distinction, but it is one that I find necessary if I am to focus my comments. I am deliberately excluding all types of libraries, whatever their organizational context, even those, if any, that may consciously have the purpose of support from income for their services. I am deliberately excluding any governmental organizations whether or not their support comes from sale of products or services.

Precise though I wish that definition were, there are still substantial problems. For example, inclusion or exclusion of the publishing activities of professional societies and nonprofit corporations is by no means clear, since the decisions they make may or may not be determined by organizational priorities rather than purely by economic, market-driven considerations. The bottom line, though, is precisely that: the scope of the private sector is determined by the degree to which the decisions are determined by market forces.

Definition of the "Profession"

Second, I am faced with equally serious problems in defining the scope of the "profession," whose views I have been asked to present. My perspective and views are based, first and foremost, on my experience for the past twenty-five years as faculty member and, for fourteen of them, as dean of a library school. I therefore must see the profession in those terms, and I immediately face the problem that its definition is by no means clear-cut. Indeed, to a large extent it now encompasses entrepreneurs and staff of private sector information agencies as well as librarians.

Just to illustrate, this past year we placed half of our graduates in industrial environments--25 percent in special libraries and 25 percent in nonlibrary contexts--with the other half going into public and academic libraries, again almost evenly split between the two. A decade ago, industrial placements were one-third and in special libraries, but growth in non-library placements has been spectacular to the point that, for the first time, we are reporting them as a separate category. Which of these professionals am I going to speak for, since they are all important to me? Views of the information professional working in the private sector as I have defined it are as important as those of the information professional working within government or in libraries.

My own professional and educational commitment has been to bring all aspects of the profession into harmony and effective cooperation, each respecting the others while maintaining its own integrity and excellence. My focus is on the librarian as professional.

For the purposes of this talk, I will present my own views of the librarian, even though doing so limits the definition of the profession. I will not attempt to discuss economic considerations.

The Professional Context

What are the bases for the professional perspective? Library professionals are concerned with the effect that policy decisions will have on the imperatives, commitments, and operational realities that are the context for professional service. They are especially sensitive to what they perceive as attacks or artificial constraints on them.

The Professional Imperatives

The librarian has two professional imperatives: preserving the record and providing access to the record.

Underlying these is the view that the record of the past is important and has value to the future sufficient to justify the cost of preserving it and providing access. I see these imperatives as comparable with those of the physician to preserve life and provide access to medical care, and of the lawyer to preserve justice and provide access to justice: they are not only professional justifications; information has value to society and the individual just as life and justice have value to society and the individual.

Information is so important to the individual that we may need to establish a public policy, as Dick Rowe suggested in his comments, for at least a "subsistence level" of information availability for every citizen. Such a policy was debated during the deliberations of the Public Sector Private Sector Task Force of which I served as chairman. While the decision was not to include such a recommendation in our report, many-- including me-- felt it was a crucial concept.

Libraries and the closely related archives are the institutions that society depends upon for preservation of the record. If they do not meet that imperative, what organization will? All experience shows that the private sector will not and, for economic reasons, perhaps even cannot. We have innumerable examples to illustrate. When books go out of print, the printer and even the publisher have no wish to be responsible for ensuring that they continue to be available; motion picture producers have universally ignored the interests of the future in their production, discarding and destroying films with abandon; television shows have reused tapes of their programs, writing over the only record of them, doing so for immediate cost savings. These information records have been preserved only because individuals and then libraries or archives have recognized their future value and importance.

Libraries in the United States at least have taken the responsibility for providing access to the records they have preserved. This is the basis of justification for catalogs and for the entire array of procedures instituted within libraries for that purpose. It is difficult to visualize any other agency taking over this responsibility, at least for the holdings of the libraries and archives themselves. But will this imperative continue to be the domain solely for libraries and archives? That is a most important question today, especially in the context of the potentials for electronic distribution. We have examples of proposals for electronic storage of records at central locations, under management of private sector organizations rather than libraries, for on-demand access. We even have examples of new means for publication in electronic form. I will comment on this later in this article.

Corollary Commitments

Given the professional imperatives, there are several evident commitments within the profession that serve as substantial determinants of its responses to policy issues. I view them as natural consequences of the imperatives, since they are natural continuations of the underlying view that information is important. Certainly these professional commitments are not limited to the librarian, but the librarian has given special emphasis to them: open availability of information, free service, and cooperation.

There is a long-standing commitment in the library profession to the open availability of information. The librarian sees information as a societal good and sees any limitation on its availability as a barrier to gaining the benefits from that good. As a natural consequence of that view, there is a long-standing professional commitment to "free" services, in the sense that the individual user does not pay for them but society or organizations do.

There is a professional commitment to cooperation rather than competition among libraries and librarians. This is exhibited in the practices in interlibrary loan, in the development of networks within states, in the development of supporting agencies such as OCLC, RLIN, the Center for Research Libraries, and in formal agreements such as the Farmington Plan. Cooperation is an evident consequence of the combination of professional imperative--preservation and access--with the economic and operational realities.

Operational Realities

Though I am focusing on the professional vision, we must recognize economic and physical realities. It is impossible to preserve every record, so selection is a critical professional responsibility. Any library must limit the range of users and uses to which it provides access; otherwise the responsibilities it has to its source of funding would be eroded. These realities make cooperation a necessity. Libraries leave to other agencies (such as the bibliographic utilities and the indexing and abstracting services) the creation of many of the tools for access. The reasons are almost purely economic; it would be impossible for each library to afford these tools of access.

Open availability to information is subject to constraints of privacy, national security, organizational interests, and economic limitations. The commitment to free service is subject to constraints--in institutional policies, in the availability of financial resources, and in the need to allocate resources effectively--but it is a commitment that must be made. Cooperation, while it may be a professional commitment, frequently becomes a burden rather than a help, which must be balanced with institutional priorities.

On balance, the imperatives and corollaries I have identified serve as driving forces in determining professional priorities. The effects of policy on professional imperatives and corollary commitments will be the basis on which I will judge issues related not only to the role of the private sector but also to that of government. We need to consider the effect of any policy upon these imperatives and corollaries, even though one may need to weigh the issue in terms of other imperatives that may be imposed upon the professional ones.

The Philosophy and Role(s) of the Private Sector

What are the counterpart imperatives, corollaries, and operational realities for the private sector?

Philosophy

I have the view, with all due respect to Milton Friedman, that private sector organizations are not "in business to make money." They are in business to meet societal needs. The private sector imperative is that it makes money as the means by which it assures that it can and should continue to meet the societal needs on which it is focused. The societal needs for the private sector information industries are evident, and I have already alluded to them as the fundamental rationale for libraries: Information is important to both society and the individual.

I have observed a number of publishers, information entrepreneurs, private sector database developers, service providers, and indexing and abstracting organizations. Each of them is clearly and rightly motivated by economic rewards. But each of them has as deep a professional commitment to the value of "information" as does the librarian. There are many ways to make money, most of them far easier and more financially rewarding than packaging and distributing information. These information professionals have chosen the private sector information industry not just to "make a buck" but because they believe it is important. Interestingly enough, the two motivations are mutually interrelated. The very value that information has is likely to be reflected in the willingness of people to pay for it. The information professional makes the judgment that the value warrants the risks and the returns will be commensurate.

Judge Posner has postulated the view that the First Amendment is merely a reflection of economic interests. I not only find that view personally abhorrent but totally at odds with the true motivations of those who depend upon that crucial part of our Constitution. It is not economics interests but political and noneconomic needs that it supports. Of course economics is important, but it is not the determinant; it is simply one of the measures.

The Roles

What then are the roles of the private sector information industry in meeting societal needs? There are two major categories, with more specific roles within each: (1) as a source of publications, in the identification of potential publications, in the packaging of information, in the marketing and distribution; (2) as a "value added" processor, in the production of indexes and abstracts, in the analysis and presentation of information, in the provision of information services.

The publisher's role is to identify authors, work with them in the development of manuscripts, and market their books. A major and very speculative investment is risked by the publisher in fulfilling this role. The relationship to the market is surely the most significant private sector concern. One cannot survive without products that can be sold. This kind of risk taking is surely the finest example of the contribution of the private sector.

The role of "packager" is equally important. Books, journals, databases, CD ROMs, films, and videos--whatever the medium may be, the information needs to be properly fitted to it. Every information company must develop the means for transforming the sources of information into marketable packages. The process of packaging is a second major investment, perhaps less speculative than that of working with the creative aspects of content, but still a major element of risk.

The publishing industry has developed a magnificent, well-tuned means for distribution. The automated components of the information industry are still struggling to establish a counterpart. To the extent that the mechanisms of advertising, promotion, and distribution function well, the information industry will prosper and the needs of the consumer will be well served.

To these traditional functions in information creation, packaging, and distribution have been added a wide range of others identified generically as "value added" services. In general terms, they are examples of information creation and packaging, but based on derivative products. The production of indexes and abstracts, with such publications as *Chemical Abstracts, Science Citation Index,* and *Excerpta Medica* as specific examples have been central to private sector information industry interests. For these, the role of the private sector is more mixed, as I will explain in more detail later.

The provision of products and services in data analysis and presentation is less well recognized, but it probably represents market potential orders of magnitude greater than the indexing and abstracting publications. Here the value of private sector risk taking is evident. Identifying market needs for information derived by the processing of available data, developing the means for satisfying those needs, and marketing the resulting products and services--these are all clearly valuable private sector responsibilities.

Those are merely one context in which information services are appropriate roles for the private sector. We see an increasing number of entrepreneurs serving as "information brokers," drawing on the resources of other private sector information companies, governmental agencies, and libraries. They fill the need for effective means for marketing and distribution for the electronic media. They also provide significant means for tailoring information resources to the needs of the market. In that respect they relate closely to libraries representing customers, partners, and potential competitors.

Among the potential services is that of electronic "library," with on-demand access and one-at-a-time publication, to which I have previously alluded. I speak of this as "potential" because it is still largely experiment, promotion, and rhetoric. Still, it represents an important new dimension of private sector services.

Relationships within the Information Profession(s)

The library profession recognizes that there are ties that bind and issues that divide it from the private sector information industry.

The Ties that Bind

Without question, the most central fact is that libraries depend almost completely upon the private sector for their collections and for the tools for access to them. Their collections come overwhelmingly from commercial publishers, with professional societies a secondary source; governments are a minor source. In this respect, the library profession sees the private sector as partners. One need merely enter the exhibit area at any meeting of the American Library Association and observe what the librarians do there.

The tools for access also come overwhelmingly from the private sector. The number of exceptions is almost minuscule in comparison. One must search carefully to identify any but the most evident examples. Even the most evident one--the cataloging data from the Library of Congress--is accessed through private sector agencies, not public ones. Of course there is the example of the products and services that the National Library of Medicine has been mandated by congressional legislation to provide. And there is NTIS, which is also mandated by Congress to provide distribution of federal government documents.

The views of the library profession concerning the importance of the private sector with respect to these support tools are evident. There may be disagreements over rights and privileges and there may be debate over technique and details. But overall, the library profession sees the private sector as an essential partner.

But how does the library profession view its relationships with the private sector in the light of the imperatives, commitments, and operational realities? Clearly the library profession regards the information industry with great respect, as an essential partner in meeting societal needs for information. Everything that can be done to increase the productivity of the private sector, the quality and diversity of their products, and accessibility to those products is all to the good. The impression in the library profession that there is not a reciprocal degree of respect and interest in effectiveness is not greatly material, but it does diminish the feeling of partnership.

That brings me to the corollary to the dependence of libraries upon the private sector. It is the reverse dependence of the private sector on libraries. First, for a wide range of publications and especially for scientific, technical, and professional ones, the libraries of this country represent from one-third to two-thirds of the total market. One study that I did of the sales of major publishers of those kinds of books showed that 40 percent of sales went to libraries, either directly or through distributors. Of even greater importance is that those sales represented the break-even point for the publishers, so that "library sales" covered the risks of the publishers. Libraries are a primary market for major categories of publication.

Libraries frequently provide the information industry with the basis for a pilot test of general markets. I think especially of the development of the CD ROM as means for information distribution. Initially, the major distribution was of library-related databases. Data shows that at least 25 percent of CD ROM publications have primary value to libraries rather than to end users. In the early days of online reference database access, libraries--especially the medical libraries of the country--provided the context for pilot test of such services.

Certainly libraries provide a crucial component of the means for distribution of private sector information products and services. With respect to the online database services, they still represent a disproportionate share of total sales.

How does the library profession view this side of the "partnership?" I frankly feel that the rhetoric of the information industry has ignored or diminished the importance that libraries have for it. The result is a perception that, if there is a partnership, it certainly is not an equal one. The libraries bear the burdens with little or none of the benefits of partnership. They are merely accepted as another market, no more or less important than any other. Fortunately, the fact that the private sector treats the library profession as a captive market has little direct effect upon the imperatives, commitments, and operational realities except as they are exhibited in the issues that divide, to which I now turn.

The Issues that Divide

Despite the common philosophical basis for agreement, there has been a remarkable number of issues that have served to divide the library profession from the private sector information industry. Without attempting to be exhaustive in covering them, I want to focus on five that I think deserve specific attention: pricing, copyright, government information, demands on libraries, and competition with libraries.

Pricing

The economic pressures felt by libraries during the past decade have been exceptional and the pricing policies of the private sector information industry have been a major element in the crisis. Libraries are clearly seen as captive markets and prices can be set by publishers at whatever the market will bear. The result has been forced policies of "deacquisition," especially of journals. The argument of the private sector companies appears to be that the availability of their publications from libraries depletes their other markets, since users will go to the library rather than purchase their own. I suggest that this view does not reflect the reality and that libraries in no way diminish the market. Discriminatory pricing will become self-defeating.

Copyright

Copyright may not be, as it once was, an immediately rancorous issue. The data clearly demonstrated that library photocopying is not and never has been a significant factor in reduction of publisher's sales. Yet for years the library community was subjected to attack, both verbally and through legal avenues. It was used as the "stalking horse" for the publishing community to deal with the much more vital and significant effects of industrial photocopying.

The problem, of course, is that the attack on "fair use," now fortunately resolved by legislation, was an attack on the fundamental imperatives of both preservation and access. Libraries were attacked for their own photocopying to preserve their collections, and they were attacked for providing facilities that aided access by the users. This had a special effect on the commitment that access be free to the user. It posed overwhelming operational problems if libraries had been forced to engage in some artificial accounting procedures. Fortunately, that is now, for the moment at least, behind us, but in my mind, the ill will shown by the publishers still rankles.

Government Information

The most central and critical divisive issue, today and for the past decade, has been the divergence in views concerning government information. To that issue I bring specific views, reflecting my experience as chairman of the Public Sector/Private Sector Task Force for the National Commission on Libraries and Information Science. I would like to review the recommendations from the report of that task force, with emphasis on their applicability to the situation today. I will do so with special attention to the views of the library profession, as I see them.

The recommendations were:

- In favor of open access to information generated by the federal government.

- In favor of reliance upon libraries and private sector organizations (both for-profit and not-for-profit) to make readily available information that can be distributed by the federal government.

- In favor of a leadership role for government, rather than a management role.

- In favor of limiting direct government intervention in the marketplace.

The view was that "private sector investment is essential if there is to be enhanced access to and wider dissemination of information."[1] On the other hand, it was also the view that government had clear responsibilities for information functions in collection and distribution. Of special importance in my view was the recommendations concerning pricing policies. These were to the effect that prices for government information "should reflect the true cost of access and/or reproduction. . . . Specifically, that means that prices should not be set to recover the costs of creating the data in the first place."

The principle underlying these recommendations was that information, from whatever source but in particular from the federal government, should be readily, easily, and widely available. Libraries and private sector companies wishing to acquire and provide access to those data, to market and distribute them, to add value to them in packaging or processing, to combine them with other data should find it easy to do so. The investment made by the government should be regarded as a national capital investment, with prices set to encourage and not discourage use of it. By making government information readily available and by pricing it at the lowest possible level-- just the cost of access and reproduction--that result could be expected.

But in the years since then, the policies of government have perverted the recommendations. Of special concern are three specific policy directions. One is pricing, the second is reduction in availability, and the third is "privatization." Libraries have seen the prices of government information, even directly from the government, skyrocket. Some forms of data have been priced at levels that make it impossible for libraries to acquire them. There have been increasing limits placed on the availability of information, by whatever means and at whatever price, from the federal government. These are matters of direct concern.

I was delighted to hear recently that one planned revision to A130 would require that prices be based on the marginal costs of access and reproduction. That would make the task force recommendation the effective basis for pricing.

The effect of pricing policies upon the imperatives, commitments, and operational realities of the library profession are self-evident. As prices are increased--in some cases by orders of magnitude--it becomes impossible for libraries to fulfill their imperative of preservation; they simply cannot afford the cost of acquisition. Fortunately, there is the depository library program, and expansion of that could serve to assure the preservation as well as adequate access to governmental information.

But the matter of deepest concern is the pressure from the private sector to force the privatization of federal government activities of all kinds and information activities--even federal libraries--in particular. The library profession sees the Government Printing Office, National Technical Information Service, the three national libraries, and the other federal libraries as vital sources of information. It looks to the depository library system as one means for assuring that the records from those organizations are preserved and made accessible.

My view is that privatization will adversely affect every principle of the library profession, that the arguments for privatization of federal information activities are invalid, and that the penalties paid by privatization will be severe. We are seeing those effects in the contracts that make federal government information available only through single source private sector companies, able to set prices at levels totally irrational when compared to the costs of access and copying--surely the most insidious and least justifiable concept in privatization. The result for libraries is a further reduction in the availability of federal government information.

This pressure to privatize is most clearly exhibited in the report of the Grace Commission (The President's Private Sector Survey of Cost Control). High among the array of recommendations of the Grace Commission were those concerned with "optimizing the use of the private sector." That section of the report reads as follows:

> Government manages best those things that are closest to its traditional functions of providing for the general welfare and security. There are numerous functions and services currently performed by the federal government that could more efficiently and cost-effectively be performed outside. However, congressionally imposed limitations on transferring functions to the private sector, opposition from federal employees, and a lack of centralized, systematic, and continuous concern have resulted in a continuing expansion of the government's commercial activities. PPSS concluded that privatization and contracting out provide significant cost savings opportunities, and recommends establishment of a central executive branch authority to identify and facilitate work toward their realization.
>
> In FY 1983, the government spent $38.9 billion in the specific areas covered by PPSS recommendations, with spending estimated to increase to $209.8 billion by the year 2000 if present policies are continued. Implementing PPSS recommendations would reduce spending to $145 billion in 2000, a saving of $64.8 billion, or 30.9 percent.
>
> Privatization involves the transfer of an activity, or part of an activity, currently performed by the federal government to a private entity. Privatization increases efficiency by targeting government resources to those activities best performed by government while turning over to the private sector those activities that can be more efficiently performed outside of government. . . . Many of the services provided by the federal government could be provided more effectively and at less cost by the private sector. The government, by directly producing services that could be produced in the private sector, creates a separate, uncompetitive market with no pressure to control costs.

It is relevant to note that the majority of information activities of the federal government are a direct consequence of Congressionally mandated requirements and governmental responsibilities. In this respect, the court ruled (National Anti-Hunger Coalition vs. Executive Committee of the President's Committee) that "It appears to the Court that these three policy recommendations are substantive in character because they affect established statutory rights. . . . While it is of course true that cost savings can always be accomplished by repealing legislation that grants specific benefits, recommendations designed to accomplish such repeal do not fall within the narrow area of cost and management control but fall directly into areas of general policy import. Such recommendations could not have been approved under the act except by a committee "fairly balanced" to represent the points of view affected, and this Committee was unbalanced as to these substantive legislative issues. In taking action on these recommendations, the executive committee did not respond in accordance with the requirements of the act and hence its approval was ultra vires and illegal because of the lack of fair balance."

Among the specific areas covered by PPSS proposals are the following relating to information products and services:

- Less government involvement in processing and disseminating LANDSAT satellite data. Selling the unprocessed data, which are commercially used to create maps and charts, to private firms for processing and distribution could save operating costs and increase revenues by $47 million and $450 million, respectively, over three years. PPSS recommended that the Government sell the rights to process, price, and commercially sell this raw data to the private sector.

- The National Oceanic and Atmospheric Administration's (NOAA) weather radio station. This could save $11 million over the three year period.

- Research activities at the National Bureau of Standards (NBS) and the Federal Trade Commission. This could save $50 million over the three year period.

Each of these, in one way or another reflects what I consider to be an irrational approach to the process of decision about how to handle federal government information. Each of them would abdicate an identified governmental responsibility. These and similar efforts have been the avowed policy of the executive branch, despite the ruling by the courts concerning the legality of the Grace Commission procedures.

As I have said, the privatization issue has been the most divisive and is seen as having the most dramatic and adverse effects on the ability of libraries to acquire and to preserve. It destroys the ability to provide access, it destroys the commitment to free service, and it destroys open flow of information. The library profession, apparently unlike the private sector, sees the federal government as a partner rather than a competitor. It is a primary source of vital information that libraries must be able to acquire and provide access to. To the extent that the private sector will facilitate those processes of acquisition and access, more power to it. But when the private sector strives to reduce that availability, it became not an aid but a barrier. In sum, the lemminglike rush to privatize adversely affects every principle of the professional librarian.

Demands on Libraries

A divisive issue of much less dramatic significance is the demands that the private sector place on libraries and especially on the major academic and public research libraries. These are the repositories of the primary literature--the journals, the reports, the documents, as well as the books--that ultimately must be provided in support of the vital functions of the information broker, the information industry entrepreneur. Use of these libraries for these functions clearly is a valuable one to society and the economy, certainly consistent with the corollary commitments of libraries. But it is not consistent with the institutional responsibilities, certainly of the academic research libraries. Their responsibilities are to the faculty and students, in support of research and teaching.

Clearly, the mere use of these resources is unlikely to interfere with the primary responsibilities, but the wear and tear on the collection, the demands for other kinds of support, the preemption in some cases of materials that are needed for institutional purposes does interfere. Recognition of these effects leads libraries to consider fees for private sector use, and that is understandable given that the use has the intent of producing income. But this has become a divisive issue in some situations.

In particular, the workload placed by private sector entrepreneurs adversely affects preservation through increased wear and tear. It adversely affects the ability of libraries to provide access for their primary constituencies. On the other hand, it does assist the open flow of information and is to that extent consistent with the commitment to free service, but still it does adversely affect many of the operational realities.

Competition with Libraries

I conclude with an issue not of so much significance today but certainly of concern in the future--the potential of competition between the roles of the private sector and those of the library. Much of the rhetoric of the private sector has implied that the library profession is a competitor to the private sector. Certainly it is a means for distribution and to that extent the private sector sees it as reducing the market for direct sales. It also serves, as I have pointed out, to open up markets otherwise not available. On balance, the view of the library profession is that the private sector has more to gain from libraries than it loses in any reasonable interpretation of "competition."

The reverse side is potentially of real concern to libraries. It is represented currently by the experiments, to which I have referred, such as Apollo, in providing commercial services for "on-demand" publication of materials, especially of journal articles. The electronic stores from which such services would be provided become the functional equivalent of libraries as means of preserving those materials and of providing access to them. Some have described these electronic files as "the library of the future," with those libraries that store only books becoming relics of the past--museums of paper, like those of papyrus and clay tablets.

Leaving aside for this essay the issue of a "paperless society" and of whether a fully electronic system will replace print in the future, this kind of rhetoric hardly improves communication with one's professional colleagues. The fact is that libraries have been at the forefront in development of electronic media for information access. They have served as the testing ground, both technically and in the economic and marketing decisions. To set up the picture of private sector enterprise becoming a competitor of libraries rather than, as I have tried to suggest ought to be the picture, as partner is I think detrimental to both players on the information stage.

Conclusion

I want to conclude with the caveat with which I started. There is no way in which I can "see" for the profession, whatever definition it may have. The views I have expressed are personal, reflecting a deep commitment to all aspects of the information profession and my own views of the proper roles of government and the private sector. I respect the political process by which through government we balance societal priorities--even though I may disagree with specific results. I respect the value of risk-taking and responsiveness to the needs of the market that reflect economic criteria--even though I do not regard them as the means to deal with all decisions.

I see the relationships among government, libraries, and the private sector as an essential partnership in which each should respect and respond to the others. As far as libraries and the private sector themselves are concerned, they need each other and their common cause is of far greater import than any or all of their differences.

Note

1. National Commission on Libraries and Information Science, Public Sector/Private Sector Task Force, *Public Sector/Private Sector Interaction in Providing Information Services*, (Washington, D.C.: GPO, February 1982), xiii.

PART 3
The Librarian and Information
Specialist View

The Government Documents Depository System

STEPHEN M. HAYES

Associate Librarian, Reference and Public Documents
University of Notre Dame
Notre Dame, Indiana

In this address I will summarize what the depository system is, how it began, and where it is now. I will also highlight some of its problems and propose some solutions.

Beginnings

"Before the establishment of designated depositories, or any systematic method for the distribution of public documents, special acts were passed for the printing of a sufficient number of copies of the public journals of the Senate and House for distribution to executives of the several states and each branch of the state and territorial legislatures. Provision was also made at the time to supply these journals, the acts, and sometimes the documents and reports to each university and college incorporated in each State. . . ." In a resolution of 1857 the Library of Congress and the Department of State were relieved of these duties and the Secretary of the Interior was charged with "distribution to such colleges, public libraries, athenaeums, literary and scientific institutions and boards of trade or public associations as may be designated to him by representatives in Congress. . . ." Later in 1859, an act was passed providing for "keeping and distributing [of] all public documents." This act charged the Secretary of the Interior with "receiving, arranging, safekeeping, and distributing of public documents 'of every nature' already and hereafter directed by law to be printed or purchased for use of the government."

In 1869 another act created the post of superintendent of public documents in the Department of the Interior. In 1895 the laws concerning printing were codified and a new post within the Government Printing Office was established. That was the Office of the Superintendent of Documents. The act of 1895 charged the superintendent with all the familiar duties for which the position is now responsible--collecting, indexing, cataloging, distributing, selling, and so forth.[1]

Where We Are Now--Description of the Present System

In 1859, prior to the official establishment of the depository libraries, about 105 libraries received publications. In 1904 about 341 official depository libraries existed. At this time a little over 1,000 documents were distributed to each. Today, there are approximately 1394 depository libraries in all fifty states and every territory. Twenty-three percent of these depositories are in public libraries; 55 percent in universities and colleges; with the balance in special libraries, such as court (7 percent), and law school (11 percent) libraries. We have expanded our services from serving a population of 82,166,000 in 1904 to 237,019,000 in 1984.[2] The ratio in 1904 was one depository per 783,000 people, to one depository per 171,000 in 1984. The amount of information handled has also changed. In 1904 there was one document per 783 people, at the present there is one paper document per 15 people and one fiche per every 13 people.[3] In 1987, 18,910 documents were distributed in paper while 23,271 were distributed in fiche.[4]

The titles distributed to those early 1859 libraries were usually congressional publications, *Congressional Record*, journals, and so forth, as well as other materials considered vital to our democratic process. The publications begun in the earlier years continued with the formal establishment of a depository system in 1859 and expanded to include geological materials as well as charts of the new territories. Today the scope of the government's interest and purview is directly represented in the breadth and diversity of the materials. New materials have been added representing executive agencies and the judicial branch. Publications now include popular titles, such as reports on the national parks and AIDS. Recently, the Department of Energy reports were added allowing contractors in universities and local businesses to access information in their area. The expansion of the geological survey begun in those early years continues today with the inclusion of the maps of the geological survey into the depository library system. In short, if the federal government is interested in a topic, there is probably information in the depository.

The Role of the Depository System

In the 1983 *Congressional Record,* in the final reading of the depository bill, when a senator volunteered to restate the purpose of depositories, several senators agreed that was unnecessary, that it needed no clarification. Unfortunately, it did need clarification; the system's role is not clearly stated. The *Guidelines for Depository Libraries* states that this role is "to make U.S. Government publications easily accessible to the general public and to insure their continued availability in the future."[5] The *U. S. Code* outlines the qualifications but implies the role, stating that an institution is suited to be a depository library only when if is "able to provide custody and service for depository materials and [is] located in an area where it can best serve the public need. . . ."[6] In the 1986 annual report of the GPO, the Assistant Public Printer again implies a role in describing his responsibilities. "The Assistant Public Printer (Superintendent of Documents) is responsible for a broad range of government information dissemination programs and services through the sale of government publications, the compilation of catalogs and indexes of government publications, the distribution of publications to depository libraries as required by law, and reimbursable mailings."[7]

None of these statements clearly defines the role of the depository libraries. What, then, can be said about it? First, the depository library program is the repository or site that allows the public to use the information their government has prepared. No one has to travel to Washington, D.C., to use this information. Second, it is a curator who collects, arranges, and organizes information for use by the public. Information without an organization is unusable, regardless of the location. Third, it is a facility where resources are not only collected and stored but where the process of facilitating takes place, making information usable. This facilitation may be as simple as finding a title on a shelf or suggesting a source that will meet a user's needs, or it can be as complex as contacting an agency concerning information not in the depository but available in such places as the Bureau of the Census's state data centers.

Problems

Depository Diversity

Depository libraries are diverse; each has its own budgetary problems, its user demands, and on-site resources of equipment and staff. In some cases this is a blessing in that we can be quite creative in solving a variety of problems. But unfortunately there is a lack of clear expectations in either direction. There is no contract stating specific instructions and requirements of depository libraries concerning service, space, and staffing. We can rarely agree upon one solution to any problem. We can barely agree on procedures.

The GPO, our parent institution, provides few "requirements" except those with regard to procedures in dealing with the GPO. Yes, we do have to fill out our forms thus and so. But in our responsibility toward the public, there are only guidelines, "recommended guidelines" at that, which convert into suggestions. The Joint Committee on Printing through the GPO has instituted some expectations, but again they are not very specific. In essence, the depositories are required to treat documents as they do any other part of their collection, providing as much access, support, and reference assistance to it as to any other part of the collection. I am not sure how well known this is to many of the depositories and most of their administrators.

The point I would like to emphasize is that the depositories lack a clear voice. We have been rather ineffectual in communicating or influencing the important decision makers. We have no true representative group for depository libraries and librarians. The Depository Library Council is appointed by the GPO to advise the GPO but has recently been expanded to represent interest other than depository libraries. Without a true voice, we are left at the mercy of those who are well organized and articulate, willing to spend significant amounts of money telling legislators what is correct and proper.

Information Overflow, Rising Expectations

The 1907 GPO annual report described depositories' problems as follows: "The libraries now designated are in many instances unable to afford either the shelf room to accommodate the books or the clerical labor involved in properly handling them. The consequence is that volumes with pretty bindings or attractive titles are taken out from shipments and placed on the shelves, and the remainder are dumped in attics or cellars. ... This sort of thing will continue so long as the Government insists upon forcing upon libraries quantities of books which they have no need. ... [N]o one knows what contingency may arise to make interesting in a locality or section of the country certain public documents which at the time of issue are of no interest or value, seemingly. Besides, public documents as reference works should be easily available, all of them."[8]

Depository libraries numbered 341 in 1904 and received a little over 1,000 documents.[9] Their problems have not changed. Today we still receive materials that may sit on the shelves, unused for long periods of time. Where we once worried about shelving, we now worry about fiche cabinets. The promise of electronic format aiding in solving our space problems has been replaced with the need for computer disk space or equipment.

The expectations of the depositories and the public are too high. We expect that everyone in Washington knows and follows Title 44, and they expect that all government reports quoted so freely in our press and news are already in the depositories. Dan Rather tells us about a report one night and

70

the public expects it to be available the next day. We expect the report in fiche in six to eight weeks. Perhaps we do not expect it at all because the agency bypassed the requirement or just forgot. But there is still the complaint of receiving too much material. I have very little sympathy for this information overflow problem. We agreed to be depositories and if we are receiving too much, then perhaps we need to reassess our participation in the program. As noted in 1907, we do not know when a seemingly trivial piece of information will become a treasure.

The GPO is doing an excellent job of identifying "popular titles of newsworthy interest" and rushing it to the libraries. The present fiche contract fiasco, however, is intolerable. The Iran-contra report issued by Congress should have been sent to all depositories in paper with the fiche edition following later when the contract problem was settled. Instead many libraries were forced to purchase copies to meet depository demand. A service driven organization (as claimed in the 1986 GPO annual report) should have made proper arrangements to meet the customer's needs, that is depository distribution.[10]

Federal Information Policy

The United States has no information policy. Instead it has a complex mishmash of regulations, laws, and customs that constitute a patchwork quilt of informational practices. This is possibly our greatest problem. Everyone talks about the public's "right to know," but it is not clearly documented anywhere.

As information becomes more and more important to the individual and society, the potential to use information as a weapon or instrument of public policy increases. The GPO in its 1986 annual report voices this new thinking with tremendous implications for the depositories. "GPO began over the past two years changes which will restore GPO to its traditional status as the natural vessel for information policy execution for the federal government."[11]

Early in the Reagan administration it became evident that information and information policies were prominent agenda items. President Reagan imposed a moratorium on the production of new audiovisual aids and government materials because too much was spent on public relations, publicity, and advertising.[12] What the depositories saw, however, was the decrease of publications and journals that were research oriented and anything but self-serving. For example, the *Car Book,* obviously an advertisement for the Transportation Department, or the *Federal Statistical Directory* from the Commerce Department are gone--at least from the government publisher. *Employment and Training Report of the President* is no longer published by anyone. The *Treasury Bulletin* is now quarterly instead of monthly. What started out as a search for waste has turned into an excuse to curtail the publication of unpopular or expensive titles or titles wanted by the private sector.

Once information was viewed as a right, unless a demonstrable need necessitated its withholding. Now, an agency is required to publish and disseminate only that information directly related to its mission.[13]

Furthermore, under the guise of economics and management of an important national resource, the means of collection, storage, access, and dissemination of information are being restrictively defined. Under the rubric of this management, we recently have the OMB advising, or rather instructing, the Bureau of the Census as to what questions should be asked during the 1990 census. This same agency is evaluating the appropriate sample size of the 1990 census. I question the role of a budgetary office advising the nation's statisticians on what is to be considered satisfactory, appropriate, or accurate to be measured.

Some have commented that under this management scenario, we have reduced the usefulness of our nation's statistical information to the point of questioning the validity and reliability of the information. Another area of this management is dissemination and access. The present thrust of policy is to emphasize access, usually with a fee, and downplay actual dissemination. As a dissemination point, depository librarians have seen resources decreasing. My library has experienced a 25 percent decrease in the number of titles received.

GODORT as well as many depository librarians, are on record concerning the lack of dissemination requirements within OMB circulars and regulations. Our comments and concerns have noted little change in the final rules, however, with only superficial inclusion into introductory or supplementary materials concerning agency regulations regarding information.

Access, as a substitution for dissemination, is only beginning to hit the depositories that traditionally have not charged users fees, especially for documents, but that cannot afford to absorb access charges to federal information along with other rising costs. When calling agencies for materials or information, I must now ask how I can acquire this material and be the judge of whether or not I can absorb the cost, or refer the patron directly to the agency so they [the patron] may assume the costs. Patrons have asked, "Isn't this government information and isn't it supposed to be free?"

Electronic Information

Clearly related to the new information policy and another of today's key issues is the effect of the electronic technology upon information, particularly information in the depository libraries. I find this area to be most perplexing and frustrating, centering around the idea that information in electronic format is totally different from the traditional sources of information (i.e., print based) and therefore outside the statutory purview of the depository library system. The depository libraries are caught in a catch 22.

Driven by shrinking budgets and regulatory requirements, the federal information producers are rapidly moving toward a paperless society for information sources. The use of electronics is not necessarily being sought for its efficiency to the agency in carrying out its work, certainly not for it efficiency to the public in using the information but, perhaps solely, because it's cheaper or more easily controlled. Here again, as with the general agency information policies, there is the failure to take into account the ability of the public to use information or provide for the dissemination of this information in the traditional sources, that is the depositories. These issues are not firmly and unquestionably established in our regulations or policies. They are mentioned but are not defined with the same vigor as are the economically based criteria.

Depositories are no stranger to electronic information. Through the use of the bibliographic utilities such as DIALOG and BRS, many of the online bibliographic and a few numeric datafiles have been used. The fees associated have been paid by the end-user or library. Another example is the CD ROM technology. While several products are now available and in use in libraries, there is some reticence to give or distribute electronic products already present in the agencies to the depository libraries. It seems we are not sophisticated enough to use these materials or we do not have the equipment. It would have been nice had the same reticence been shown with fiche technology. Instead, it was distributed, and the libraries had to cope.

Many libraries now have the capability to use electronic information and should be able to select that material already available within agencies. The current pace seems to be predicated on the ability of the depositories or the GPO or someone to come up with the ideal plan for electronic information implementation. I refer again to the fiche distribution. A well-covered plan was not evident then, and yet depositories coped and it proved to be the savior of many a GPO budgetary problem---simply send it in fiche!

Electronic information is different and cannot be distributed until a well-thought-out plan is in place, and a well-thought-out plan cannot be in place without some electronics in the depositories. To add to the problem, a very well-organized group is on record opposing direct distribution of electronic information by GPO. Much emphasis has been placed on the wording of the 44 USC 1901 defining "government publication" as "informational matter" that is published as an individual document at government expense, or as required by law. Yet in the H. Rpt. 90-1719, the committee addressed the fear in this way: "It is sometimes feared that the mere changes in terminology and style will result in changes in substance and impair the precedent value. . . . The statute is intended to remain substantively unchanged."[14] I interpret that to mean government information regardless of form, that is, public documents of "all manner," such as books, maps, and charts, mentioned in the 1907 annual report of the public printer, and would now include electronic information.[15] The question is not whether electronic information is a government publication, but what is the most effective method of incorporating the electronic documents into the present depository system. Further delay reduces the resources that the public has had available to them for well over a century. It is poor service to keep denying them this information.

Privatization

With the Reagan administration, a new agenda arose--privatization. The Reagan administration believed that the government should not compete with the private sector and should allow the private sector to do what it does best--let market forces produce the best information product at the cheapest price. I have no problem with the privatization concept except when it has a negative effect on the depository system.

Recent OMB regulations require agencies to produce only that information (1) required by their mission or law, (2) not now produced by the private sector, and (3) not likely to be produced by the private sector. Unfortunately this leaves most information on the table and ripe for picking.

I do not have any problem with using the private sector as a source for supplying the depositories with government information. I do object to replacing cost-free access to government information in the depositories with pay-as-you go private sector products. For example, a private company produces indexes that cover congressional and statistical materials all of which are, supposedly in the GPO's *Monthly Catalog*. An interpretation of OMB Circular A-130 could require the GPO, if it were an executive agency, to cease indexing these materials since *Monthly Catalog* "competes" with these private sector products. The regulations and philosophy do not consider the historic precedent of *Monthly Catalog* nor that the private sector is a late arrival in the indexing field. What has happened is that more materials being taken over by the private sector and then the agencies are expected to cease producing the information.

I would propose a partnership, nonexclusive toward either party. The private sector can and should be used as a contractor to product information, products for distribution to the depository libraries. This continues the tradition for citizen use of government information in the depositories. This contract would be through GPO with severe penalties for any default. (Our present six-month fiche crisis with a private sector contractor, which has all but stopped depository distribution to fiche selecting libraries, should warn the politicians against considering the private sector as a panacea.) Once this "basic information product" is available in the depositories, the private sector can take the same product or information, enhance it, and sell it. Citizens who can afford the enchanted product can make use of the private sector product. Those unable to afford the private sector product can use the depository basic information product and derive the same information with perhaps more effort.

Examples of such materials already exist today with our indexing systems. Our library spends $18,000 each year on private sector information products related to depository materials. I do not expect this to decrease. What I expect is that the depositories will always be the "safety net" for the economically deprived who cannot afford private sector products. In other words, there will always be a *Monthly Catalog*. So if CIS overprices its indexes, or my endowment funds dry up, we can still access congressional and statistical materials.

Those who see the private sector as the altruistic supporters of free access to government information are perhaps misled. The public policy goals of the information sector include a fair and open marketplace in which to compete; a marketplace that encourages diversity and ensures intellectual property rights of information companies and their customers; the prevention of restrictions that impede the ability to compete and prosper; the opposition of restrictions on the individual or businesses to acquire information; and primary reliance on the private sector.[16] There is nothing about democratic institutions or the right of free access to government information. The private sector expects to make a profit, as it should. But this should not be done at the expense of the public, which has already invested in the production of this information.

At a recent meeting concerning the privatization of NTIS, the question arose of how quickly unprofitable segments of NTIS could be dropped by the private sector. I think this indicates the direction the private sector will take in safeguarding the information resources of the government.

In his book on the GPO, Kling states,"A joint resolution known as the Printing Act of 1819, attempting to bring some semblance of order out of the chaotic situation which had developed under the low bid system . . . laid the groundwork for twenty-seven years of unprecedented profit for printers fortunate enough to be supplying government printing."[17] Many fail to remember that in part the GPO was created to correct this situation. I foresee a similar period of unprecedented profit taking by the information sector. We are simply replacing the print media with private sector electronic, and, we may have twenty-seven years to wait until Congress again corrects the situation.

The Future: Parallel Worlds

I read science fiction almost exclusively, and a popular theory in that genre is that of parallel worlds. For every choice another parallel world is created. In one world, for example, Rome never fell and the earth is different for it. Let me present three parallel worlds of information.

In "world one," a prospective library user would be provided with almost all of the information needed. He or she would be able to use INFONET, developed by Omni/Info for the government and distributed by the GPO along with laser disks. The disks would be updated periodically by accessing the computers at the GPO Data Center and sorted using ULTIMA from DATAboys. The user would be able to obtain hard copy or a floppy, or the information could be read directly into his or her computer file. There would be no charge to the user because all government information is free. There would be a charge for association data because the association's files are private.[18]

The library user in "world two" would start by using INFONET, but it would be a long and effortful process because in this "world" the library would not be connected to the GPO Data Center. Information that previously was collected by the GPO would not be owned by the private sector and there would be a fee to use it.

A "world three" library would have paper and fiche information available to the user, but most current information would be electronic and there would be a charge for using it. The computer would be able to tell the user how much the service would cost, and if the user could not afford it he or she would have to file for a waiver and wait ninety days or more for a response because the federal government is so busy and understaffed. In "world three" your choice would be to use old paper and fiche titles or apply for a waiver.

Which world will we see in our future?

Notes

1. Robert E. Kling, Jr., *The Government Printing Office* (New York: Praeger, 1970), 33-34.

2. Joseph McClane, 25 March 1988, telephone interview, Library Programs Services, Government Printing Office, Washington, D.C.

3. Government Printing Office, *Annual Report of the Public Printer for the Fiscal Year Ended June 30, 1906* (Washington: Government Printing Office, 1907), 352.

4. McClane, telephone interview, 1988.

5. U. S. Government Printing Office, *Guidelines for Depository Library System* as adopted by the Depository Library Council to the Public Printer, 18 October 1977 (Washington: Government Printing Office, 1978), 1.

6. "Public Printing and Documents," *United States Code*, Title 44, Pt. 1909, 1982 ed.

7. Government Printing Office, *Annual Report of the U.S. Government Printing Office, 1986* (Washington: Government Printing Office, 1987), 18.

8. Government Printing Office, *Annual Report of the Public Printer for the Fiscal Year Ended June 30, 1906* (Washington: Government Printing Office, 1907), 353.

9. Ibid., 352.

10. U.S. Government Printing Office, *Annual Report of the U.S. Government Printing Office, 1986* (Washington: Government Printing Office, 1987), 1-2.

11. Ibid.

12. Federal Audiovisual Aids and Publications (statement, 20 April 1981), *Weekly Compilation of Presidential Documents* 17,no.17 (27 April 1981): 447.

13. OMB Circular A-130.

14. U. S. House, 90th Congress, 2d session, *Enactment of Title 44, United States Code, "Public Printing and Documents"* (H.Rpt.90-1719) (Washington: Government Printing Office, 1968) (serial set 12795-5), 2.

15. Government Printing Office, *Annual Report of the Public Printer for the Fiscal Year Ended June 30, 1906*, 351.

16. Information Industry Association, *Public Policy Activities of the Information Industry Association, June 1987* (Washington), IIA, 3.

17. Robert E. Kling, Jr., *The Government Printing Office* (New York: Praeger, 1970), 12.

18. Greg Bear, *The Forge of God* (New York: TOR, 1987), 320.

Resource Sharing through Networking

WILLIAM DEJOHN

Director, MINITEX Library Network
Minneapolis, Minnesota

Richard De Gennaro calls the effect of technology on libraries a "revolution in access to library resources by users." He wrote that "technology is making the resources within a library available beyond its walls, and the resources beyond its walls available within the library."[1] This revolution in access is occurring as we meet together to discuss effective access to information. How we meet the challenge of this latest revolution will dictate in many ways the future role of the library in society.

Let me illustrate this revolution with three examples.

1.   Current online catalogs are raising expectations of users as they begin to find out what information is available in their libraries. Library users of the online catalogs are spreading the word to non library users to come see what can be found in the library. When the system is down, few people go to the card catalog, a librarian's tool. They leave and come back when the system is available again.

2.   The University of Illinois Champaign/Urbana Library Circulation System model, where patrons view holdings of other cooperating libraries and can charge out items from terminals, thereby bypassing interlibrary loan offices. This will be duplicated by other local systems if it has not already. It will create policy questions--do we want to empower our patrons with that much authority? I predict this will be a trend in other systems. My staff

already search the LCS remotely and request materials on a daily basis.[2]

3. The OCLC New Reference System--due at the end of 1988. OCLC is cloning its 17 million record online database, adding indexing and software to it including full boolean capabilities and making it available through dial access or dedicated OCLC terminals. The target audience is academic staff (faculty-students) in higher education institutions. Holdings will be available though it has not been decided how they will be displayed One idea would be to take the three-letter OCLC symbol and translate it to institutional names; end users can access via dial up and pay by credit card. *End user* in this context means not only you the librarian, but also you the patron. Far fetched? Not really. Western Union now offers INFOMASTER, which can be accessed by credit card and has online help available and will even perform the search for you. OCLC is putting up a one million record database to begin using a test reference database. The same software will be placed on their current CD ROM databases, ERIC, AGRICOLA, and Science and Technology. A user can dial into the online reference service from local CD ROM database searches to check on current information.

    This is not an advertisement for OCLC, but to illustrate that soon faculty members and possibly many other current library users may have access to the OCLC database and maybe they can request an article online from the *Information House* if it takes too long to find it through their local library--they may not even have to come into the library.

These are but three examples that I believe illustrate the revolution in access we are experiencing. The speed at which this access occurs is unbelievable. The first two examples are now operational and the third example is being tested within the next few weeks with a database of one million records from the current OCLC online database.

At this point, the technology is here and will be implemented. How successful or effective this increased access will be to some extent depends upon library policy makers and how effectively staff are trained to handle the growing inquiry from our user and non user populations. The user has greater access than ever before. This will have an effect on current policies. This is something we will have to deal with and I am not sure many of us have thought it through--I do not believe users will accept the answer that we have never done it that way before.

The planners of this conference posed the following question in their brochure: Is resource sharing basic to access to information or is it an ineffective substitute? In my opinion, resource sharing has always been basic to access to information and will continue to be so. It cannot be a substitute for having the information requested available to the user when he or she requests it.

Resource sharing can be an effective level of access to information when the material or information is not locally available. Libraries practicing effective resource sharing can make it possible to provide access to information; as F. William Summers said in his essay "The Need to Know," the "least important" citizen, the citizen who cannot afford to purchase information, the citizen who needs information and is not quite sure how to go about finding it--that citizen should be able to contact his or her primary local library and obtain access to resources that will satisfy his or her needs and interests in a timely fashion. Similarly, the "most important" citizen should be served equally well. Our users should not be penalized because their library did not purchase something that would have provided them needed information.

With greater electronic access sometimes the most effective way to obtain information, libraries will have to deal with how to carry this out in an equitable manner so as to provide that needed access to the "least important" and "most important citizen."

The Library of Congress Network Advisory Committee in 1987 issued a statement, *Library Networking: Statement of a Common Vision*. Part of the basis for this statement was a desire to promote the concept of "'the Nation's Library' as the aggregate of all available information resources." The statement points out that "our common vision of networking is an environment in which libraries can provide each individual in the United States with equal opportunity of access to resources that will satisfy their and society's information needs and interest."

To reach the goal of "'the Nation's Library' as the aggregate of all available information resources," information must be available to our users when they contact their library either in person or by remote access. This access should be supplemented by networking and effective resource sharing protocols and methods when those resources are not available.

Let me share a recent definition of network with you: "A network is a formalized structure to facilitate exchange of information and services and to promote development and transfer of new services in the library field. The word network in the library field carries the connotation of cooperating membership, resource sharing, linkage, and use of new technologies."[3]

When I use the word *networking*, I am speaking very broadly of the techniques libraries are currently using to cooperate and share resources among themselves to improve services to their users. Networks includes OCLC, RLG, WLN, SOLINET, the states of Florida, and North Carolina, and the Triangle Libraries.

Let me briefly describe how we in the MINITEX region--Minnesota, North Dakota, and South Dakota--are trying to provide effective resource sharing for scholars, researchers, and users of libraries. We stress users of libraries because that is the business we are in: delivery of information for users through their local libraries. It is as important that the user in greater Minnesota have access to resources in a timely fashion as the user in the Twin Cities. The scholar or research in Grand Forks and Fargo, North Dakota, was recruited by the presidents of both universities on the basis of having efficient access to the University of Minnesota research library collections. It is important because these individuals cannot drive across town to the Twin Cities libraries. So our services were established with timely service to the user as a very important part of the service.

The MINITEX Library Network offices are located in the main library of the University of Minnesota Libraries. The university is a member of RLG and of OCLC. It is also a regional depository with a full document collection. MINITEX is funded by the states of Minnesota, North Dakota, and South Dakota. No fees are charged to libraries. Rather then give you a history of MINITEX, let me briefly explain what we now have in place in the region and how we are trying to make effective resource sharing through networking.

Figure 1. MINITEX Mission, Goals, Services, and Functions

Mission

MINITEX is a publicly supported network of academic, public, and state agency libraries working cooperatively to improve library service. The mission of MINITEX is to enhance the effectiveness and efficiency of all participating libraries by expanding their access to state, regional, national, and international library resources., This is accomplished by sharing library resources, including collections, bibliographic records and holdings, and reference services through the use of both conventional and innovative procedures and technologies. With this service, library patrons have much more effective access to a full range of state and regional library resources.

Goals

1. Facilitate the resource sharing activities of its participants.

2. Provide and offer leadership and expertise to participating libraries and other public bodies in furthering interlibrary cooperation and innovation.

3. Provide a forum for ongoing planning of interlibrary activities.

4. Provide access to bibliographic records for the participants.

5. Cooperate with other groups and agencies with similar goals and activities.

Services and Functions

1. Operate a document delivery service.

2. Operate the Minnesota Union List of Serials program.

3. Offer and support on-line shared cataloging services and related activities.

4. Operate a backup reference service.

5. Cooperate with the University of Minnesota in the operation of a serials exchange program.

6. Communicate to all constituencies information on MINITEX programs and policies.

7. Provide a forum for training, continuing education, and professional development relevant to the services and functions of MINITEX.

8. Identify and facilitate consideration of current technologies and innovations which may affect library cooperation.

Resource sharing is broadly defined in our region, with special emphasis on sharing staff knowledge and expertise. *Information* is broadly defined to include library resources and any resource that provides information. We spend a lot of time speaking to nonlibrary staffs about libraries, networking, and resource 'sharing. It is not uncommon for me to attend a breakfast sponsored by METRONET, one of our multitype library systems, and have the majority of the persons at my table be connected with local government in the Twin Cities. They are vitally interested in knowing what libraries do, in networking themselves in order to share information, and in working together to provide access. Figure 2 provides a detailed description of MINITEX services.

Figure 2. Description of MINITEX Services

Interlibrary Loan

The MINITEX office receives and fills loan and photocopy requests from participating libraries using first the collections of the University of Minnesota Twin

Cities Campus Libraries and other libraries in the Twin Cities. Other requests are referred electronically to libraries throughout Minnesota, North Dakota, and South Dakota. Reciprocal agreements allow access to libraries in Wisconsin and the University of Illinois at Champaign/Urbana. Requests are also transmitted to the Library of Congress, National Library of Medicine, National Agricultural Library, and the British Library Document Supply Centre.

Online Catalog of Books and Other Materials

Over 155 libraries in the MINITEX Library Network contribute their records to OCLC, a national online database maintained by the Online Computer Library Center in Dublin, Ohio. This allows the libraries to share their resources with one another and with over 5,000 libraries throughout the United States and Canada. MINITEX staff provide training and support for OCLC services in the region.

Union List of Serials (MULS)

The MINITEX office maintains MULS, a list containing holdings of magazines and periodicals owned by libraries throughout the network. This computerized union list is being loaded into the OCLC online database and will be updated regularly. MULS is used by all the MINITEX libraries to share resources among themselves and with other cooperating libraries.

Serials Exchange

Over 350,000 duplicate and discarded magazines and periodicals are processed annually by the MINITEX staff to supply participating libraries with issues needed to fill gaps in their collections. This is the only source for some libraries for such needed items.

Skills Development

Workshops, seminars, and training sessions are provided by MINITEX for local library staffs throughout the network. This provides opportunities for staff members to learn from one another and to discuss ways through which new technologies and mutual resources can be used to provide better service to library patrons.

Reference and Associated Services

The MINITEX office provides backup reference services to Minnesota public libraries through a contract with the Minnesota Office of Library Development and Services and to other participating libraries in obtaining discounts for online and CDROM reference databases and tape processing services.

Document delivery is our most used service, making heavy use of the University of Minnesota Twin Cities campus library collections and the Minneapolis Public Library collections. In 1986-87 we processed over 183,000 document delivery requests, or about 850 per day. Were we effective? It is up to the local library user and library staff to make that judgement. Effectiveness is in the eyes of the requestor. I know we can do better, and we constantly are asking ourselves how procedures can be streamlined to get information to the user more quickly. Over 62 percent of the requests are filled from the University of Minnesota and the Minneapolis Public Library collections, and the majority of those requests filled in seventy-two hours or less and put in our delivery service. What cannot be supplied by the university collections is referred electronically to other holding libraries in the region, usually within twenty-four hours of the decision to refer. We make heavy use of the private college consortium in St. Paul (CLIC) and of other libraries in Minnesota, North Dakota, South Dakota, Wisconsin, and the University of Illinois at Champaign/Urbana.

The academic libraries in the region are probably 90-95 percent retrospectively converted into OCLC, so we have a fairly good hit rate when searching for monographs. The use of the (MULS) Minnesota Union List of Serials and OCLC and the local delivery services provides effective access within smaller communities to wanted materials.

Regionwide Delivery System Operated by MINITEX

The MINITEX office operates a regionwide delivery system consisting of overnight couriers, UPS, and first-class mail into major communities with concentrations of libraries.

In 1979, the Project for Automated Library Systems (PALS) was initiated to help Minnesota's institutions of higher education meet their growing demand for specialized information resources. Today, PALS is supported by state appropriations through the Minnesota State University System Board.

PALS has an online catalog for students and faculty and for dial up access by the communities. The state universities share dial access phone numbers with their local communities, including schools. Part of the mission of these institutions is to serve the community, and access to the library's online catalog is an important part of this outreach. PALS now has, in addition to the online catalog, an integrated circulation system; an interlibrary loan system similar to OCLC's ILL subsystem; a serials control system; an acquisition system; and many other developments

PALS is a subset of the MINITEX Library Network. MINITEX staff actively helped in the development of the interlibrary loan subsystem, receiving requests that cannot be filled from other PALS libraries first and referring to PALS libraries for materials not available at the university.

South Dakota has purchased the PALS software from Unisys and has received state appropriations for hardware to operate a statewide network involving its higher educational institutions and the South Dakota State Library.

In North Dakota, the North Dakota State University has been a member of PALS since its beginning because of unique relationships with other academic institutions in the Fargo/Moorhead area. The University of North Dakota has received funding to purchase a local automated system and PALS is one of the systems it is considering.

The University of Minnesota Twin Cities campus has an online catalog using NOTIS system, and MINITEX uses a system called LUMINA. The university received a grant from a private foundation to finish its retrospective conversion of all its holdings, and one proviso was to provide access to LUMINA for MINITEX participants. MINITEX will be providing training to participant staffs on the use of the university's online catalog.

The CLIC libraries--private college libraries in consortium in St. Paul--have the Carlyle online catalog in a joint database. CLIC is one of the largest users of MINITEX and is used by MINITEX as a major referral source, since we have twice daily delivery between the MINITEX office and the CLIC libraries.

MINITEX and State Library Joint Standards Review Task Force

The task force has been meeting since 1981 and has published minimum standards for local online catalogs and circulation systems, including a Bar Code Directory to prevent community libraries from duplicating bar code numbers. We have also published minimum standards for bibliographic input and encouraged libraries to have dial access ports on their local automated systems. We just passed a resolution that has broad support stating that online search-only access to bibliographic databases in automated library systems will be available at no charge to designated nodes in statewide library resource sharing networks such as MINITEX or PLANET, the public library network.

Dominant Themes in Networking

Charles Hildreth identified three themes dominating the changing environment of computerized library networking and automation in North America:[4]

1. The centralization/decentralization issue.

2. The lure of local integrated systems.

3. The trend toward local resource sharing.

The Centralization/Decentralization Issue

According to Segal, networking efforts in libraries have been shaped by forces pulling toward centralization and forces pulling away from it. Prior to 1980, one of the major reasons MINITEX libraries joined OCLC was to develop a regionwide database. The thought was that someday we would somehow have a single, unified three-state database of monographic and serial holdings to facilitate resource sharing. In 1980, the library leaders in the region stated that we probably would not have such a database, and, in fact, the disparate databases that existed at that time (the University of Minnesota Twin Cities, PALS, and the more than 5 million records in OCLC) formed the regional database. So we concentrated on resource sharing protocols, delivery mechanisms, training, and a commitment to building our database in OCLC and moved toward local integrated automation systems.

The Lure of Local Integrated Systems

The second theme of local integrated systems became noticable in the region with libraries seeking to purchase local systems. We held several regional conferences on automation developments and commercial vendors began having a great impact as they exploited low-cost minicomputer technologies and offered affordable turnkey automated systems. MINITEX libraries began installing local integrated systems. Of course, they could not communicate with one another. In 1984 when I arrived at MINITEX, I believe there were only three local automated systems in the region--DRA in the Southeast Library system in Rochester, CLSI at Hennepin Co., and PALS in six state university libraries. Today, three-and-a half years later, there are nine different local integrated systems in operation involving over seventy MINITEX libraries.

The Trend toward Local Resource Sharing

The trend toward local resource sharing has occurred at the local level within the MINITEX network. The PALS libraries began in 1984 to share monographs among themselves using the PALS intelibrary loan system before sending a request to the MINITEX office at the university. But the loaned books continued to move through the MINITEX delivery system. Today, about 4,000 books are loaned among the PALS libraries in this fashion. Local resource sharing was a dominant theme because of the existence of MULS, the union listing tool, and OCLC. The addition of local automation accelerated this trend, especially among the cities where state universities existed because they provided dial-up access to their local collections. So local resources, encouraged by local delivery systems, are being used in an efficient manner.

For example, in the Fargo/Moorhead region, there exists the Tri College organization: Moorhead State University, North Dakota State University, and Concordia College in Moorhead. Through Tri College, students and faculty at each member college have direct access to the resources of all three college libraries. They may visit any of the three libraries and check out materials, but they may also use only their home school library and have materials delivered from the other two libraries on a twice-daily shuttle. That shuttle service is partially supported by MINITEX. All three libraries are members of PALS and share not only a single computerized catalog but also a computer based union list of serials. There is an intercampus bus service, and Tri College recognizes minors earned through the student course exchange. The three college libraries are currently exploring the possibility of developing a standalone miniframe PALS system to include the three public libraries in the Fargo/Moorhead area. If this is accomplished, this would be the first move to decentralize the PALS system on a local basis with a gateway link to the mainframe PALS database in Mankato. MINITEX remains the document delivery link with the rest of the state's libraries and also provides other services currently, such as OCLC support. Since I believe the PALS libraries obtain about 50 percent of their current cataloging from OCLC LC MARC records and 50 percent from member contributed records in the OCLC database, I do not detect any movement away from using OCLC as their source database for records in the near future.

This theme of local resource sharing has always existed in the Twin Cities public library system, MELSA, with a shared title listing for monographs and serials. Now that all nine public libraries in the system have automated local systems, they are carrying out dial access experiments with one another.

South Dakota's library network based on the PALS software establishes a statewide automated network with the majority of the public and academic libraries committing themselves to joining the network. There is only one other local automated system in South Dakota--Dynix in Sioux Falls Public Library--and it will tapeload records into the South Dakota Library Network database in order to participate in resource sharing.

So the dominant themes identified by Hildreth are occurring in this region as they are throughout the United States and Canada. Fortunately, MINITEX has not established its own automated system. We are concentrating on facilitating the sharing of resources and keeping everyone up to date on what everyone else is doing and providing other regionwide services. Through the Joint Standards Task Force, we are now beginning a series of educational sessions on the Linked Systems Project to determine the best way to provide whatever will be necessary to link those systems that logically should be through some dedicated mechanism. In my own mind, I am not convinced that everyone has to be linked to everyone else. It may be easier to link the university's LUMINA/NOTIS system with the state university's PALS system and the several Carlyle systems in private colleges. Once this occurs, it will probably automatically include the libraries in South Dakota and North Dakota on the PALS system, since they will be linked sooner than anyone else because they use the same software. Among the academic community this is taken for granted, and only the timing and method seem to be in question. MINITEX's funding through the higher education board and the traditional cooperation among the academic libraries make this possible, though there will be policy issues to deal with. Among the public libraries, with so many different systems, we will have to make a determination as to how far linking should go. Our standards already call for dial-up access.

A major change in MINITEX with all this linking will deal with the delivery system that is now a hub through the MINITEX office. Everything comes in and out of the office, since all courier services are initiated there every afternoon. This linking will mean that material should be moving directly between local communities rather than traveling through the MINITEX office. This will be a major change in South Dakota, which does not have a statewide delivery system at this time. All of this will require additional funding.

You should be aware that the PALS system retains the OCLC record number, and we believe that it will not take too much effort to link the PALS interlibrary loan system with the OCLC interlibrary loan system. Several academic libraries with local systems are eagerly awaiting OCLC's development of a connection between their systems and the OCLC database. At the proper time, there will be closer linkages facilitated by the fact that MINITEX itself is an OCLC regional network office that happens to operate a major regional resource sharing program. That will mean that our services will become even more efficient and effective, with only one input of a request that will automatically route throughout the region and then move to a national level as appropriate. Given the fact that on the average MINITEX is filling 84 percent of PALS requests right now in an average of seven days, which includes referral time to other libraries, we believe the remaining 16 percent can be routed nationally at a greatly reduced turnaround time for the patrons. It is conceivable that the PALS interlibrary loan subsystem could be the dominant system in the region.

I believe most of these efforts will occur in the next two-to-five years. The technology is either available or will be available soon. The basis for resource sharing and cooperation through networking is traditional in the region, and we have a solid base to build upon. It is natural for all of us to move forward. The university continues to be a dominant resource sharing partner in the region. Since MINITEX is part of the university libraries, we have the opportunity to help plan how libraries in the region can have access to the special databases that one day will be available through the university's computer centers. We also will help the libraries in the state become a dominant voice in the state of Minnesota to ensure that the university libraries receive the collection development funds needed not only to meet the needs of its primary clientele but also to serve as a major resource for the state and region.

Conclusion

Resource sharing through networking is alive and well in the upper midwest region, and I am sure there are similar stories occurring throughout the states and provinces of North America. I note, however, that outside our region we still use the library rate to send material across the nation. Within states and regions, we have our own delivery methods, but nationwide delivery is poorly coordinated. I doubt that electronic access or facsimile transmission is necessarily the only answer, since some needed resources and information cannot be sent economically using this method.

Our challenge is to meet our user's individual inquiries on his or her schedule of need, not on our schedule according to our procedures and practices.

If the other stakeholders at this conference make access available and dissemination effective, we will work at the local, state, and regional level to make that information available to the general citizen.

Notes

1. Richard De Gennaro. *Libraries, Technology, and the Information Marketplace: Selected Papers.* (Boston: G.K. Hall, 1987), 11.

2. Bernard Sloan. "Resource Sharing among Academic Libraries: The LCS Experience," *Journal of Academic Librarianship* 12:26-29.

3. Teresa Strozik. "The Linked Systems Project--From the View of Networks--Implications for Librarians." *Smart Presentation*, New York Library Association October 1987, 1.

4. Charles R. Hildreth. "Library Networking in North America in the 1980s," part 1: "The Dreams; The Realities," *Electronic Library* 5, no. 4 (August 1987):25-26.

The Fee or Free Dilemma

JOHN N. BERRY, III

Editor, Library Journal

Most Americans would subscribe, as I do, to the belief that we have historically stated as Jefferson did: "That Government is best which governs least." Even if it governs least, however, we Americans like our government to be accountable, obviously small, and close to home.

In economic terms we would probably agree with the corollary assertion that "Government must not intervene unless the marketplace fails." This is a dictum we hear incessantly from business, and currently, from government, or at least from the executive branch. I actually agree with it, however, and I think most Americans do. Let me state it again, and use it as one point of departure for this discussion of the fee or free dilemma in information service and in libraries. In my view, when we discuss fees for library service we are discussing important barriers to the citizen's right to know. In any case, I would stipulate that government must not intervene unless the marketplace fails.

We have just seen the final year of an administration and a president of unprecedented activism in the pursuit of those two ideas, a government that governs least, and a ubiquitous marketplace, unrestrained by government. It is a marketplace into which we try to force every human need and desire in this society. Our very value system, that is, the measures by which we label the relative value of nearly everything are, as a result, economic, and for the most part, in this market dominated society, boil down to dollars.

We all probably agree with those two general statements about government and the marketplace; indeed they describe and even define free enterprise capitalism: "Government must not intervene unless the marketplace fails." One result of our unity in support of free enterprise capitalism is that there are very few socialists, communists, or fascists in our body politic. Our most bitter debates, our worst arguments tend to be well contained within the parameters of the free enterprise system. When we are faced with a failing economy, with economic disaster, even then we do not radically alter our system. We simply shift our collective view of what constitutes marketplace failure, our view of what requires government intervention. Instead of a socialist revolution, we created the New Deal. There were, of course, some Americans who labeled the New Deal socialism. Others realized it prevented socialist inroads in the United States.

Even today the argument, stripped of its emotion, is simply a discussion of what constitutes marketplace failure; interestingly enough even Adam Smith, the economist who, legitimately or not, sired most of the theory that is capitalism, described certain areas in which the marketplace was never going to work, never going to succeed. Smith was a true believer in free trade, and not only did he want that free trade unfettered by any interference from the state, but he also wanted it unfettered by corporations and by monopoly. Smith still believed in a role for government and saw government's role as particularly important in a free society. Let me quote him:

> Though the state was to derive no advantage from the instruction of the inferior ranks of people, it would still deserve its attention to see that they should not be altogether uninstructed. The state derives no inconsiderable advantage from their instruction . . . they are more disposed to examine, and more capable of seeing through, the interested complaints of faction and sedition, and they are, upon that account, less apt to be misled into any wanton or unnecessary opposition to the measures of government. In free countries . . . the safety of government depends very much upon the favourable judgment which the people may form of its conduct it must surely be of the biggest importance that they should not be disposed to judge rashly or capriciously concerning it.

Smith even elaborated on two kinds of educational institution that represented ways the state could legitimately intervene, as he put it: "those for the education of the youth, and those for the instruction of people of all ages." Smith gave a definition of education as a public good that still works for today's economists, and I quote again: "the expense of the institutions for education . . . is . . . beneficial to the whole society, and may, therefore, without injustice, be defrayed by the general contribution of the whole society." These theories of Adam Smith, who died in 1790, are very much a part of current applied economics and give us a definition of a "public good," as opposed to a commodity or private good that stands the test of time very well.

Now in my view the verbs "instruct" and "inform," though not exact synonyms, certainly overlap in meaning. Even that great free enterpriser Adam Smith stipulated at the outset that "instruction" of both youth and people of all ages was a legitimate responsibility of government because it benefitted the entire society. He agreed with us that education, and by extension informing the citizens, were public goods because when anyone in the society took advantage of them the whole society benefitted.

Why don't we provide these so-called public goods in the marketplace, but in fact, don't we do that sometimes now? Yes, we do, but we believe that education must be equally accessible to all, at least up to a certain level, and we do argue about what that level is. We realized centuries ago that the marketplace could not handle that mandate to inform all, to educate everyone. So we turned that job over to government. In some jurisdictions government intervenes all the way through graduate schools, while in others it quits at the end of high school. What is interesting, though, is that whenever we have spotted education needs that the marketplace did not provide like those remedial community college programs that cover our national landscape, we had to bring government into the picture to provide them.

Libraries were founded on the same basis. My favorite example is the justification for the founding of the Boston Public Library. It is clear to me that the founders of libraries, particularly public libraries, based that act on their view that libraries are educational institutions and clearly exist for the instruction of people of all ages, including youth. In 1852, sixty-two years after Smith died, the trustees of the Boston Public Library realized the need for a public library, because the many private libraries that flourished in Boston then did not do the job, were a marketplace failure because, as those trustees put it: "multitudes among us have no right of access to any one of the more considerable and important of these libraries," and, "except in rare cases, no library among them seeks to keep more than a single copy of any book on its shelves . . . no one of them, nor indeed, all of them taken together, can do even a tolerable amount of what ought to be done towards satisfying the demands for healthy nourishing reading made by the great masses of our people, who cannot be expected to purchase such reading for themselves."[1] The trustees called those private libraries "inadequate" because they were "adventures and speculations for private profit."

But then they came to the real point:

"It has been rightly judged that--under political, social and religious institutions like ours--it is of paramount importance that the means of general information should be so diffused that the largest possible number of persons should be induced to read and understand questions going down to the very foundations of social order, which are constantly presenting

93

themselves, and which we, as a people, are constantly required to decide, and do decide, either ignorantly or wisely."

What about access? "As to the terms on which access should be had to a city library, the trustees can only say that they would place no restrictions on its use. Of its use . . . regarding it as a great matter to carry as many books as possible into the home of the young, into poor families, into cheap boarding houses, in short, wherever they will be most likely to affect life and raise personal character and condition."

They called the result, the library, the "crowning glory of our system of city schools," and would make that library an institution "fitted," they said, "to continue and increase the best effects of that system."

Since that time we have paid for this system of public libraries, the greatest such system in the world, with tax money and public funds. We add philanthropy to that funding when we can get it. Suddenly now, for a number of reasons, there is a resurgence of the movement to add direct user fees to the funding mix. Here is why I believe that would be not only foolish and inappropriate but also downright dangerous.

The first justification is that through the device of a fee we will be able to pay for services we cannot otherwise afford. While one has to agree with those who say government funds are limited, that the tax base is limited, it must be obvious that if we believe in libraries and information as public goods, as necessary to the welfare or our society and government, then they are of as high a priority as many other government supplied services and are thus worthy of tax support.

Among peoples of the world, Americans are neither the least nor the most taxed, but as a percentage of our GNP, our taxes rank very low, much less than most nations of Europe, or those economic wizards the Japanese and the Germans. Public libraries have never received more than 2 percent of the tax money collected by state and local government. They disappear somewhere below 1 percent of all taxes collected by all levels of government.

At less than 2 percent of the costs of state and local government, public libraries are clearly a bargain, serving regularly from 30 to 50 percent of the population. Surprisingly, this has been their position among government expenses for their entire history, so an almost invisible reallocation, just 1 percent more of our taxes sent in that direction would increase library support by at least 50 percent, and in many jurisdictions, double library budgets. We could probably find 10 years of that amount in the money wasted each year by the Pentagon or stolen from it.

More important, there is very little evidence that when tax subsidies and fees are combined, the result is more revenue for the agency involved. Obviously that did not work for AMTRAK, it does not work for the any commuter railroad in the United States.

Think about all those services and agencies where user fees and tax support are combined. Public hospitals are in chaos. The post office cannot compete. Public colleges, where tax subsidy and fee cross paths again, cannot pay competitive salaries, are chronically short of funds, and currently face enrollment problems as well as perennial trouble with the legislators to whom they report.

One could go on and on. The point is clear, there is little evidence out there to show that the imposition of fees actually increases the revenue. Some librarians make that happen with a certain sleight of hand, but you have to remember that the public has already paid for the building, the collection, and the salaries; to impose fees, even for those "special" services that provide electronic, or better and faster, access is charging them twice. In the case of certain online systems they may have paid three times before they get the service, since the research and development costs in many cases came out of the defense budget.

Another justification often made for user fees is that they help ration the service for which a fee is charged to those who are willing to pay. Public libraries ought not to be providing services that must be rationed. There is no reason to ration public library service. There is, after all, no shortage of information, so why must we ration it? If it is sensitive, if it must be secret, or confidential, then we can lock it up. To ration information to those who can afford to pay extra is a highly discriminatory act. It creates a barrier to access for those without the money. We do not need to ration information; on the contrary, we need to disseminate it more widely in the interest of democracy.

That immediately leads to another justification: why not let those who get the benefit, the users, pay for the information, and for the library. The reason we do not charge them for the library is that since Adam Smith, we have agreed that it is a public good, that when anyone uses the library, the whole society, everyone benefits. The same is really true of all information.

Indeed, while it must be obvious in this information society that you can make money by packaging and selling information, it is also obvious that in many ways, there is a clear-cut marketplace failure in information.

People tend to cough up their hard-earned money only for those things they want, which is why some books, not always very good ones, are bestsellers and others are in library collections (I know, bestsellers are there, too). We have always asserted, however, that in every society, but particularly in a democracy where the citizens govern, information is crucial. Knowledge is power, information is power, we say. We require education, it is mandatory, because we know all kinds would not shell out their time or money for it if given the choice. We make a certain level of education universal and mandatory. We tax for libraries for the same reason. Our society must have citizens informed and educated at least to a certain level. So even though some people will pay and pay handsomely for some information, and you can build businesses on that basis, you cannot depend on that marketplace to inform citizens well enough that they can effectively participate in self government, in democracy.

Incidently, to a surprising degree, government has had to intervene in all information packaging to make it viable. What author or publisher could profit without the monopoly given by government's laws providing copyright. What magazine could make a profit without the subsidy of second class postage? What about the library book rate?

Through our government we give information vendors, including those who produce packages in electronic formats, a monopoly called copyright on their particular package of information simply because without it they would not be motivated to create the package, and if they were, in a truly free market, it would be every publishers to publish.

Even economist Lawrence J. White, who asserts that the public "does not meet the standard criteria of a public good,"[2] agrees that "information has the properties of a public good. Once it is in existence, one person can use it and benefit from it without using it up or interfering with the benefit enjoyed by other users."[3] White also asserts that access to information qualifies as a public good: ". . . access clearly does have the properties of a public good. The extra costs for providing an additional person with access are very small or nonexistent.[4]"

Even if you agree with me up to this point, you may still harbor doubts, may hear that echoing refrain "there's no free lunch." And you may still wonder, even if they add insufficient revenue, what harm it would do to charge fees for faster, better access to the information contained in the collections of public libraries or the files and machines of government.

Evidence of harm appears in a host of ways. First, fees discourage use. When a charge was levied for access to medline, a large number of doctors, a group who could surely afford the price, simply stopped using it. That scary example has public policy and societal implications. Less dramatic, but still noteworthy, is the degree to which the use of telephone information has diminished. I do not know the precise figures, but the decrease is huge. There is simply no arguing with the fundamental marketplace truth that as the price, in time, money, or whatever increases, demand generally decreases.

There is another way, of course: make that price increase mandatory, a tax, the way we pay for education and libraries now, based on the premise that the institution needs the money to provide a growing service that qualifies as a public good, because it serves the whole society.

A more damaging, harmful effect is the impact of a user fee on the fundamental assertion that a service or agency is a public good. We are faced with this set of facts: user fees are discriminatory in that they allow you to decide not to serve a group of people, those who cannot or will not pay the fee. In our society most citizens live at the middle and lower levels of affluence. They have limited discretionary funds, and long established patterns of spending them.

The imposition of new fees on a previously free (tax-based) service effectively stops these groups from using the service, even if that cessation is voluntary. Where this has been researched, such as at a huge suburban library system near Chicago, use of online searches is much, much less in the libraries that charge fees.

The damage is just as great to the library whether people elect not to use the information or are prevented from using it because they have no money. There will be both categories among these new nonusers of libraries and information.

By imposing a fee between citizen and information, you immediately send a message to the society, including the politicians and voters, that it is acceptable that some people, either by choice or because of lack of resources, cannot and will not use the service or the information. If you can agree to that, it follows that you agree that access to that information or service is not essential. (You surely cannot defend the proposition that the ability to pay is the equivalent of need.)

It is obvious that regardless of their need for the service or information, some will not get it when you impose a fee. That is pretty good evidence that the service is not essential, and a pretty good argument for the idea that it is no longer a public good. Ultimately, this line of reasoning will lead to the place where the agency or the information service, and access to them, are deemed to lack qualifications to make them worthy of tax support.

In my view, the most serious damage done by the imposition of a fee is that it provides convincing evidence that the information or service for which you levy that fee is not sufficiently important to be provided as a societal need, but only as a marketplace want. Government provision or subsidy of that information or service immediately becomes suspect and you force it into that marketplace where the fundamental determinant of access is ability to pay.

In short, the fee sends the wrong message about the political and social importance of access to information. Interestingly enough, it sends an incorrect message about the very nature of information as well. We hear conservatives from government and the private sector claim that information has already been "commoditized." They are already claiming that it has been forced into the marketplace, where forces like competition in its provision, and the other "tests" of the marketplace are claimed to improve its usefulness and access to it. In truth, copyright really prevents true competition in information.

I do not deny some of those conservative claims, but I have to point out that the information itself, unlike the packages it comes in, is not what has been commoditized. The information, as the Federal Office of Management and the Budget learned, along with economists like White, and Getz in our own field, has none of the properties of a commodity at all. First, it is not scarce. Second, when you use it it is still there, it is not consumed. It does not wear out or ever go away. You can pack it up and sell it, lend it, or give it away and you still have it. Clearly, it is not a commodity.

When information is put in a package, or sold outline, or lent or given away, all you can really buy and sell is the package or the arrangement, because the information itself exists independent of the package or format in which it is delivered. In the marketplace, however, you have to buy the package to get the information. In truly free environments, like a library, you can use the information to your heart's content without ever being subject to those laws, rules, and tests that make up that marketplace.

Fees change all that, because they require that you pay for the package once again, but the package this time is the library, and thus that fee forces the library into the marketplace, but as an agency of government, it has no real business there, unless that marketplace has somehow failed.

On the basis of the points I have made, I conclude that government intervention in the provision of information is not only valid, but is as old an American tradition as the public library, copyright, or the capitalism first properly described by Adam Smith. The imposition of fees into that government intervention is inappropriate, is ineffective, and creates barriers between citizens who need the information to govern themselves and the information they need.

Most important, it sends a message to all that it is acceptable to discriminate between who will have access to information and who will not, on the basis of ability to pay. To discriminate at all about access to information is to endanger our citizens' ability to work, live, and, most of all, govern themselves. We must not allow that.

Notes

1. Report of the Trustees of the Public Library of the City of Boston, July 1852, city document 37, Boston, 1852, 15.

2. Lawrence J. White, *The Public Library in the 1980s* (Lexington Books, D. C. Heath, 1983), 137.

3. Ibid., 126.

4. Ibid., 133.

PART 4
The Needs of the Many Publics

Scholars, Youth, and the General Public

WARREN J. HAAS

President, Council on Library Resources
Washington, D.C.

Let me begin with the introduction to a proposal from the Council on Library Resources to the Ford Foundation. The year is 1982.

These are times of great change for all users of libraries. Computer terminals are replacing card catalogs, information is stored on optical discs as well as in bound volumes, and communication networks are expanding prospects for new and useful services while also complicating established ways of doing things. Rising costs curtail library operations even as user expectations rise, and a new economic setting for information services generally is pitting market forces against a tradition of library service as a public good.

The mix of new technologies and new economics is at the heart of the present library revolution, but that revolution has so far been most concerned with changes in internal operations of libraries--in organizational structures, in costs and funding, in staffing, and in cooperative planning. These are all important matters, and it is essential that they receive attention. But the results of such work will not be fully satisfactory and the "revolution" itself will be incomplete if the focus for action is centered exclusively on libraries as organizations. The needs of would-be users--all users--must be better understood than they are now, and the means for meeting those needs must be freshly and imaginatively considered. Libraries must operate in cost-effective ways, and they must use new technologies skillfully, but most of all they must be sensitive to the needs of scholars and students and to the full range of interests and concerns of the entire population. Equally important, they must be prepared to serve those needs as they *will be,* not as they once were. Systems, technology, manpower, and funding are means, but in the final analysis it is access to information by users that will measure the success of the library revolution now under way. It is this complicated, much advertised, but poorly understood matter that is the subject of this proposal.

Ford responded positively, marking the beginning of CLR efforts designed specifically to identify needs and to improve access to documents and information. I will report some of what we have observed during these past six years as we have sought to learn more about the needs of users and promote equitable and effective access to information--this is the only way I can approach the abstract and monumental topic I have been assigned. There is an added difficulty. I have been asked to speak about needs of three categories of individuals--scholars, the general public, and youth. Even though CLR concentrates on the academic world, I am not and never have been a scholar, I am not at all certain that there is a general public, and I do not remember what youth is.

Looking back, the council's intention to address the broad issue of access and to understand better the needs of users has not gone as we thought it might and, in fact, has proved to be more difficult and frustrating than any other of our recent undertakings. Why this has been the case is uncertain, but at least a hint came during the time I was preparing for this meeting. I came across a review in *Science* of Peter Temin's recent book, *The Fall of the Bell System.* The reviewer, William Baldwin, reflected on the author's thesis that for a half century or more, the Bell system worked extraordinarily well. But at some point, the Bell goal of "universal service" (i.e., a telephone in every home connected to every other telephone), coupled with continuing technological improvement, eventually came to be seen as a corporate responsibility to *define* the needs of users (rather than ascertaining what their customers wanted) and then to design products to meet those *perceived* needs.

If we do not carry the analogy too far, there is perhaps a lesson here for CLR and for many libraries. We have all assumed that, by and large, what libraries and librarians do is for users: the building and housing of collections, the careful cataloging of books and automation of bibliographic services, the organization of specialized collections, the provision of reference and circulation service, and so forth. There can be little argument that the needs of users are at the heart of library operations, but there is a growing feeling, especially among scholars, that the *ways* libraries do their work is determined more by management concerns than by user needs.

This may or may not be the case, but we have observed on many campuses that libraries and librarians are too often isolated from the core of academic life and are too often peripheral to the central academic structure. As a result, the remarkable progress libraries have made in many areas is too little known, the current directions libraries are taking as they shape their future are often not well understood by either faculty or administrators, and the relationships between libraries and other university components are uncertain and often fragile. These conditions make it difficult to learn what users need. To complicate the matter, most users do not know what they will, one day, need. The process of scholarship leads to needs; it doesn't stem from them. Further, projecting the future from past practice, especially in our complex and dynamic information world, is a hazardous enterprise. User studies only record past use of what libraries have offered.

With these three matters as a backdrop--the inevitable conflict between organizational practices and personal needs, the isolation of libraries and librarians, and the difficulty scholars have of projecting and articulating needs--let me review some recent efforts undertaken on behalf of the cause of both effective and equitable access and then reflect on what we have learned.

The CLR access program has had a life of its own, but its objectives have also penetrated other program areas--bibliographic systems and services, preservation, library management, the development of consortial undertakings, and even librarianship itself. As visible evidence, we refer you to the council's 1984 statement on "Scholarship, Research, and Access to Information," to my knowledge the first formal public statement by the CLR Board of Directors, and one that subsequently was formally endorsed by ALA, ARL, RLG, OCLC, IFLA, and other organizations.

During the past six years, nearly twenty formal and informal meetings on nearly as many subjects, related in one way or another to access, have been initiated or supported by CLR, and dozens of grants have been made. Examples of topics considered during such meetings are implicit in the meeting names: "Electronic Information Delivery Systems," "Access to Historical Information," and "Information Access in Historically Black Colleges." A few titles of projects funded by CLR will give some sense of the diversity: "Telefacsimile as a Means of Improving Interlibrary Document Delivery," "A Study of Information-Seeking Behavior of Ph.D. Students in Selected Disciplines," "Symposium on the Public Lending Right," "A Consumer's Guide to Databases for the Researcher: A Feasibility Study," and "An Electronic Delivery System for Images from Library to Classroom."

Limited time precludes a full description of the work done by grantees under this program, but, all in all, it has been fragmented and diffused. Even so, the emphasis has helped to install the issue of equitable access as an underlying theme of much CLR and national activity. While concentrating on access equality and system effectiveness has made these topics more visible, and while probing the subjects of needs and access from every possible angle has helped to illuminate the issues, we are still far from understanding the future needs of users; in fact, we are just now learning how to find out.

The best way to provide a status report of the search for ways to understand needs is to survey current work in this especially active period of discovery. I will use five or six examples to suggest the diversity of this effort and the elusiveness of useful results.

Stimulated in part by the difficulty of converting the cause of access to a program of action, the CLR Board encouraged expansion of the council's support for research. With funds from the J. Paul Getty Trust, the Pew Memorial Trust, and the Andrew W. Mellon Foundation, CLR established, late in 1985, a research program to explore--through analysis, research, experiment, and discussion--topics pertinent to providing and managing the information resources needed for teaching and scholarship in the future. The focus of the program is on the influence of technology and the opportunities it presents for universities, their research libraries, and the process of scholarly communication in general.

The general outline of the research program was shaped by the CLR Board after extended discussions with university officers, scholars, and librarians. The program is divided into two parts: (1) university-based analytical studies to concentrate attention on the characteristics and use of information as well as the organization and management of information systems and services within universities; and (2) a program to encourage a wide range of research by individuals. This CLR program is meant to explore the relationship between the content and form of information, especially in the context of research and teaching, and the needs of users. The goal is to point the way toward more effective and coherent planning for future information systems and services offered by libraries.

The first institutional grant was awarded to UCLA to develop a long-range strategic planning process for libraries and information resources. This work is viewed as a possible prototype for efforts in other settings. Robert Hayes, dean of the Graduate School of Library and Information Science, is the program director, and through his considerable efforts (and not without difficulty), faculty from most divisions of UCLA have been directly involved. Fifteen or twenty exploratory studies have been funded, and they have, in turn, stimulated several extensive projects of potentially great importance, including:

1. A reassessment of information resources for instruction in design, School of Architecture.

2. Planning for integrated information services, Graduate School of Management.

3. Development of an information system as an integral component of a new Hazardous Substance Research Center.

4. A supporting study for a multicampus project to produce a definitive edition of publications and manuscripts related to the voyages of Columbus.

5. A study of information needs, resources, and accessibility for a new developing countries research program.

To give recognition to the UCLA program and to encourage other universities to consider institutional research programs, CLR convened a meeting at Malibu, California, in September 1986. Library and academic representatives from ten universities were invited to hear UCLA's progress report and to discuss approaches to strategic planning. Two of the participants, the University of Minnesota and the University of Illinois at Chicago, each subsequently developed proposals in the context of the research program.

At Minnesota, faculty and library staff are developing a model for information services to be provided by the library of the Hubert H. Humphrey Institute of Public Affairs. The first phase of the project includes five studies: information requirements assessment; information technology, resources, and services forecast; organizational structure assessment; consideration of costs and funding; and a study of policy and legal issues. The second phase of the project, to be completed this year, will be the actual design of the model system.

The University of Illinois at Chicago has turned to its Institute for the Humanities as the test site for a research program, with two objectives:

1. To engage scholars on campus in reviewing how they do their research, what tools and languages they employ, and how the results are disseminated.

2. To develop, collaboratively, the long-range policies that will influence the way the library will assist in the process of scholarship.

Two librarians have joined the institute this year to study scholar-library relationships and to identify user problems that stem from library policies. A conference at the year's end will concentrate on a topic pertinent to CLR's interests and judged to be important by Institute fellows.

A more specialized project, but one of great potential importance, is the exploration of the structure of texts in machine-readable form. CLR funded Carnegie Mellon University to plan and hold a conference on this subject in May 1988 for representatives of publishing companies, library networks, and Carnegie Mellon computer science faculty members and library and information system planners.

The overall intent of the CLR research program is to encourage libraries to look ten or even twenty years into the future by learning more about needs and then to develop the capabilities required to meet those needs. At least three million dollars have been made available for support of work that falls within program guidelines and can pass a rigorous review process. But despite these initial projects, which were stimulated by council staff, the response of librarians, library school faculty, and individuals from contiguous disciplines to the challenge of the research program has been less than we had hoped.

Rather than abandon our efforts to promote research, we have sought new ways to make the program work. On the assumption that the research tradition of librarianship is not yet well established, we have moved ahead to construct a stronger foundation that will provide support and guidance. The Association of American Universities, the American Council of Learned Societies, and the Social Science Research Council have recently joined forces with CLR to create the Research Library Committee--about twenty-five scholars from the humanities and social sciences, university officers, and foundation representatives committed to bringing the needs of users and the operating responsibilities of libraries into balance with the fiscal and organizational realities of universities. The work has just begun, but excerpts from the record of the first meeting on 18 January 1988 will give some sense of what lies ahead.

As might be expected from the composition of the committee, the interests and concerns expressed concentrated on three topics: financial and management issues; needs and problems of users; and (to a lesser degree) operational practices, technological prospects, and organizational trends. I will not report all that transpired at the first meeting, but I want to give some sense of the mix of opinions and points of view by reading a series of brief statements, each of which reflects an area of substantive discussion.

1.   Financial and management issues

- Given the expectation, held by many users, of continuous collection growth, library costs are difficult to control. External forces largely determine the number and prices of journals, foreign exchange rates, telecommunication costs, access charges to database services, and so forth. On financial considerations alone, the expectation of continuous growth needs review and, probably, revision.

- Information sources of all kinds and information processing technologies are increasingly integrated. As a result, the traditional organization of universities is under stress.

- Too little information about costs of library and related activities is known, and what is known is not effectively used for management purposes. For example, what is likely to be an appropriate portion of a university budget allocated for library and information services? What effect does a given level of library expenditure have on the quality of present and long-term educational and research performance?

- Financing the library over the next five to fifteen years demands special consideration and a planned approach. The costs of innovation and transition cannot be routinely accommodated in an annual operating budget. A "political" constituency is required to make the case for public and private sources of funds.

2.   Needs and problems of users

- The technical orientation of librarians is becoming increasingly sophisticated, but they are perhaps becoming less "faculty-like" and less cognizant of user needs. The most effective faculty-library communication exists when librarians are virtual colleagues of faculty in terms of knowledge and allegiance to an academic discipline.

- Too little is known about how faculty, graduate students, and undergraduates actually make use of library resources and services or about how various factors influence their use.

- Can technology provide a substitute for close proximity to books, archives, and other scholarly resources? Can improved links to naturally related collections and information services be developed? Can bibliographic structures for the humanities be developed and maintained that will be comparable in coverage and performance to those available for the sciences?

- Universities do not generally involve faculty in making fundamental decisions. Traditional library committees do not consider important topics, perhaps because the issues are not being raised.

- As yet, there is not much evidence that scholars in the humanities are making extensive use of new automated bibliographic systems.

- Better ways must be found for scholars and universities to state their expectations and specifications for the performance of various information technologies before they are installed.

- New computer-based capabilities are affecting publishing and the methods of scholarship. Neither the benefits nor the risks of relying on these evolving systems as full or partial substitutes for print on paper are known.

- There is growing evidence of conflict between long-cherished aspirations for library self-sufficiency and the fact of increasing functional interdependence.

A number of projects to support future deliberations of the committee were suggested during the meeting. They are listed here with only slight amplification.

1. Increasingly, libraries are involved in collaborative enterprises, but there is often a mismatch between the costs incurred by contributors to such projects and the payments made by beneficiaries. What are the costs to individual institutions of such "public good" services (interlibrary loan and access to specialized collections are examples), how can such services be financed, and how important are they to users?

2. Copyright law, proprietary issues, and regulations are increasingly affecting library operations as new technologies transform the processing, storage, and distribution of information. There is an inevitable link between these issues and the economics of libraries. This subject needs evaluation against the backdrop of such requirements as equitable access to information and the conditions for doing business in the academic world, including effective management of university resources.

3. What do faculty and administrators see to be the role of the librarian? Is there great variation? How do these perceptions match those of librarians? Where are librarians in the university decision process?

4. In schematic terms, and from the point of view of users, is there an ideal physical layout of an academic research library?

5. How can graduate students understand better and become more sophisticated users of the future "model library," both for their own research purposes and as eventual teachers?

6. Can a set of models be developed to provide cost and performance projections (a) for libraries in their present form extrapolated to the future and (b) for alternate library forms that

reflect extensive changes in technology, operations, and external affiliations? What would a library for the twenty-first century, designed by users, be like?

Now let me leave the Research Library Committee and turn very quickly to other examples of efforts to discover needs. About two years ago, work was completed on a ten-year survey of the social sciences--a project sponsored by the National Research Council and intended to project the thrust of research in primary fields of the behavioral and social sciences.

In April of 1986, Sidney Verba, Director of the Harvard University Library, and I wrote to the nearly two hundred participants in the NRC project, all scholars on the cutting edge of their disciplines, to ask what information resources and services would be required for the work they projected. Only seventeen individuals responded, and even a few of those responses were routine. But there were also carefully reasoned, thoughtful letters that reflected needs and interests of the kind that must be factored into future planning.

The most prominent concern, and not a surprising one, relates to the acquisition, organization, and availability of data sets--data sets of all kinds, ranging from standard sets (i.e., census) to project-specific sets, automatically, and ideally, linked to bibliography and perhaps to the text of evaluative work. Of special importance for inclusion is the identification and description of the methodology used. One correspondent wrote from Cambridge, England, that "The challenge to libraries is to provide computer-based information retrieval services to the methodologically based, interdisciplinary consortia of researchers who will probably be responsible for the mega-projects which really advance our knowledge." Others underscored the need for collecting and organizing special categories of material ranging from publications of labor unions, special interest groups, and political parties to the field notes of anthropologists and laboratory notes of scientists.

Expert systems that would link inquiries to resources, the capacity to handle cartographic materials electronically, and computerized text storage were all identified as desirable library services. From the social sciences and the humanities, there is also a persistent call for a level of bibliographic coverage that would be, for those disciplines, comparable to the level that has been developed for the sciences. In short, librarians are being asked to turn the possible into routine practice. This ascending scale of user aspirations reflects, in the words of one of my colleagues, the assumption of entitlements unqualified by definition, by priorities, or by fiscal considerations.

A final example of forecasting techniques is one that is taking shape in the context of the work of the Commission on Preservation and Access. The commission is concentrating initially on the preservation of the content of brittle books. There are millions of titles at risk, and there is no prospect or even a need to save them all. But which should be saved? What strategy should be followed to select? The search for the answer to these questions is under way and the results are likely to provide improved understanding of the priorities and interests of users of many kinds of libraries--historical societies, those public libraries and collegiate libraries with distinctive collections, and large general research libraries. An early indication of the potential value of this approach is found in an informal undertaking of the American Council of Learned Societies. The secretaries of the forty-five constituent societies were asked to establish priorities for the preservation of materials most important to the disciplines they represent. To date, there have been twenty reports filed and it is no surprise that the aspirations are expansive and demanding: the records of science (History of Science Society); the case files of all civil and criminal cases in U.S. district courts prior to 1970 (American Society for Legal History); ethnographic artifacts (American Anthropological Association); early audio recordings (American Dialect Society); Russian, Soviet, and emigre materials, all on poor paper (Association for Advancement of Slavic Studies); secondary material from the nineteenth century, the period when advancing scholarship coincided with the growing use of acidic paper (American Philological Association, American Society for Eighteenth-Century Studies, Medieval Academy of America).

I could go on, but let me end this very selective yet, I hope, illustrative survey of our difficult and frustrating search for ways to determine future needs, and conclude with a few observations about what we have learned.

I use the term observation rather than conclusion advisedly. Not long ago I saw a sign beside the door of a Pittsburgh church that said, "I'm not young enough to know everything." As one approaching mandatory senility, the message struck home.

My first observation concerns predicting the unpredictable. There are, obviously, many levels and types of information and information needs, and many of those needs can be anticipated and accommodated. But the nature of the frontiers of scholarship and the unpredictable courses chosen by the most imaginative scholars to penetrate the record of the past, taken together, frustrate orthodox planners.

This does not mean that the search to identify future needs should be abandoned. Rather, it means that the search should concentrate less on specific needs of individuals and more on fundamental and broader questions. If we are entering a new information age, we had better learn more about it. How do information requirements vary by discipline? How parochial is the research community? How does information availability affect the methods and substance of research? What is the relationship between format and utility? Put more broadly, the field of information studies needs a stronger base of analysis and research than it presently has.

Answering such questions is not a matter for librarians, acting alone, even though the answers will redefine the library of the twenty-first century (which is really what we are considering at this conference). A purposeful collaboration is required with users of libraries and those who allocate funds if the result is to be intellectually acceptable, operationally sound, and fiscally responsible. While we librarians cannot, by ourselves, do the job, it is our responsibility to see that the job is done. There are some who would say that shaping a foundation for our profession of facts about information and its use is our greatest challenge, and possibly librarianship's last chance to flourish as an academic profession.

A second observation follows on the first. If the specific needs of individuals are difficult to project in any useful way, perhaps libraries should make whole disciplines their target, forcing those disciplines to do what individuals cannot. This approach has, for many reasons, worked well in the health sciences. It is risky, of course, to ask for advice unless one is prepared to accept it, and, pressed as they are to accomplish long-established and valid responsibilities, there is no way each library could add to its agenda the new tasks that would result from wide and purposeful consultation.

The only possible way to address this aspect of our future is through a new level of institutional collaboration--to create, in effect, that national library we hear so much about. If ten, then twenty, then thirty libraries each took on one assignment of importance, in collaboration with leaders of a given discipline, and chose methods that would take full advantage of what librarians know and what computer and telecommunications technology can do, we might well be on the way to shaping the nation's research library structure of the future. Whether collecting and properly organizing massive but specialized categories of publications, or films, or archives; whether aggregating and making generally useful privately developed data sets on one subject or another; or whether assembling a team of experts to assist an entire discipline, there is an opportunity here for a giant step forward in the definition of library service.

There are no technological constraints--when electrons are no longer fast enough, photons will take over. Further, the financial problems inherent in funding cross-institutional costs could be worked out. The problems are managerial and organizational--essentially, they are problems of will, both for the disciplines and for libraries.

Third, we should give some special attention to the role of the Library of Congress. Mr. Billington, the new librarian, has embarked on a year-long management review and planning process, one objective of which is to consider external services. There is an opportunity here for libraries and the library user community to shape public practice (as distinct from public policy) that should not be left to chance. Librarians, the academic disciplines, and leaders of research universities will have to work together, work quickly, and work skillfully to make certain that the most important of their concerns are known and heard. What the Library of Congress does in the future will affect the performance and operating costs of all libraries and the work of scholars in all disciplines.

Implicit in my remarks and throughout this conference is the message that the future is not simply an amendment to the present and past. From now on, people cannot pretend to be educated if they do not comprehend the information foundation of our world. The ways the human record of creation and discovery is generated, organized, produced, distributed, and put to use must be understood, as must the ways information can be controlled, manipulated, and misused. Young people must have their critical senses finely honed if this new thread of civilization is ultimately to strengthen ties and not weave curtains. The specific responsibility of librarians in this very special aspect of education is perhaps the greatest of all.

Finally, the needs of the general public--all of us. The record of library performance, especially during the past twenty years, has been remarkable. Computerized bibliographic systems, state and regional support and organizational structures, and even the new effort to establish an accessible collection of preserved materials are all examples of improving the effectiveness of access systems. But the cause of *equitable* access is still an unresolved public problem that the new information era will only make worse.

Last Sunday I was at St. Marks National Wildlife Refuge, walking by myself, when a formation of white pelicans flew slowly overhead, the only sound the movement of air fanned by fifty or sixty pairs of wings. After the moment was gone, I remembered that only a few weeks ago just one white pelican brought down a low-flying, 280 million dollar B1-B bomber, killing three of the crew of six. An Air Force spokesman, in splendid bureaucratic form, reminded a critical press that "after all, the pelican is a big bird."

The effective *and* equitable assurance of access to information that is needed by individuals in all settings and in all walks of life, nationally and worldwide, requires the same commitment that underpins our national security. In an era where the cost of only one fragile bomber equals the annual budget of the Library of Congress, is close to the total yearly expenditure for books of the one-hundred-plus libraries in ARL, and exceeds the projected cost of a brittle books preservation program designed to save and make accessible a large portion of the human record, we have cause to wonder about the commitment of society to the substance of the information revolution.

Somehow we have to make the case for support persuasively and honestly, and then we have to perform as we promise. The B1-B had a soft spot. In reshaping and extending the library services that have performed well for many years, we must exercise great care and show great skill. There is some risk that, unless user needs are in balance with operational concerns and are tempered by the realities of funding, the product of the information revolution will itself be dangerously flawed--an albatross for users and librarians alike.

Bibliography

Clubb, Jerome M. "Computer Technology and the Source Materials of Social Science History." *Social Science History* 10, no. 2 (Summer 1986).

Committee on the Records of Government. *Report*. Washington, D.C.: Council on Library Resources, 1985.

Govan, James F. "The Creeping Invisible Hand: Entrepreneurial Librarianship." *Library Journal* (January 1988).

"Information in the Economy." Special section in *Bulletin of the American Society for Information Science* (February/March 1988).

Lambert, Richard D., et al. *Beyond Growth: The Next Stage in Language and Area Studies*. Washington, D.C.: Association of American Universities, April 1984.

"Large-Scale Data Resources for the Social Sciences." Report of the British-American Joint Committee, prepared at the request of the Economic and Social Research Council (U.K.) and the Division of Social and Economic Science, National Science Foundation (U.S.A.). June 1985.

Nickerson, Raymond S. *Using Computers: The Human Factors of Information Systems*. Cambridge: MIT Press, 1986.

"Preservation of Scientific and Technical Literature." *CLR Reports* 2, no. 1 (February 1988).

"Reading: Old and New." *Daedelus* 112, no. 1 (Winter 1983). Proceedings of the American Academy of Arts and Sciences.

Scholarship in the Electronic Age: A Selected Bibliography on Research and Communication in the Humanities and Social Sciences. Compiled by Anita Lowry and Junko Stuveras. Washington, D.C.: Council on Library Resources, February 1987.

"Summary Report on Preservation Initiatives Among ACLS Societies." Unpublished report, American Council of Learned Societies, 18 February 1988.

Writings on Scholarly Communication. Washington, D.C.: ACLS Office of Scholarly Communication and Technology, 1988.

PART 5
Removing or Neutralizing Barriers

Illiteracy and Aliteracy

JANE C. HEISER

Administrator, Office of Life-Long Learning
Enoch Pratt Free Library
Baltimore, Maryland

There has been a good deal of discussion about access to information. The speakers have touched on the limitations that arise from problems of physical access, cost, and the lack of ability to use information. What has struck me most is the frequency of use and descriptions of the word *user*. What has pleased me most is the awareness by everyone that there are those who are information poor, that there is a less sophisticated general public, and that there are those who are illiterate and under educated. What concerns me most is the lack of understanding of the scope of the problem. Several speakers have talked about "pockets of illiterates" as though they make up a very small segment of the population. The reality of the situation is just the opposite. Believe it or not, 75 million Americans--one third of our entire population--would have difficulty understanding or utilizing the majority of the resources that have been discussed here.

We all know that the question of access has been with us since the beginning of time. Knowledge was and still is power. By limiting access to a certain few, man could control others and early on set the stage for a have/have not system. Education--the acquiring of knowledge/information and the use of it has always been looked at as the key to improving one's lot in life. Since the days of "olde" serfs, peasants, and slaves have looked at the ability to read as the first step to control their own lives and better their lot, often going to extreme measures to acquire that ability.

Democratic societies established public education and libraries. An eighth grade education became the achievement of the educated man, then a high school diploma, then a college degree plus. The movement toward a higher level of education paralleled the increasing complexity of the world around us. For a while it looked as though we were closing the gap between the have/have nots. But then came the information explosion and the gap is widening again. It requires more knowledge and skill to comprehend, respond, and participate effectively in today's world. The "user" of the past is becoming the "information poor" of the future.

The principal barrier to information in the past and present is the lack of ability of the user to be aware of the resources, where to find them, and how to use them. This was as true when the first printing press was invented as it is with the most sophisticated computer today. The key to the problem is basic--twenty-six letters.

The Problem of Illiteracy

Media, reports, and studies will tell you the problem is staggering--27 million adults in this country are functionally illiterate--that means one out of every five adults. Forty-seven million more are able to read only on the most minimal level. If current trends continue two out of three Americans could be illiterate by the year 2000. The cost of illiteracy is enormous. Billions of dollars for welfare programs and unemployment compensation are directly traceable to illiteracy. More than 60 percent of those in prison are illiterate. Those who serve this population talk about the loss of self respect, the frustration of constant helplessness, and fear of being found out.

Figure 1. Sample Findings of the APL Study

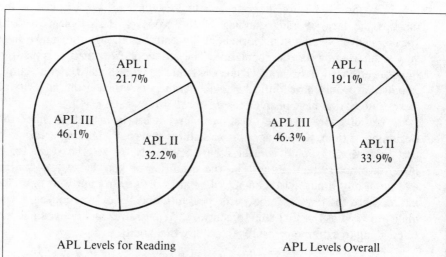

APL Levels for Reading   APL Levels Overall

The definition of functional illiteracy has been the subject of many debates. The dictionary says it is the ability to read and write--true--but it is not that simple.

The first real attempt to define or come to grips with the problem was the Adult Performance Level (APL) Study conducted in 1970 at the University of Texas at Austin. Based on a sample of adults performing on indicators that cover five general knowledge levels and four skills, the study identified three levels of competency: APL I, functionally incompetent; APL II, competent, but marginally so; and APL III, most competent. The areas of knowledge were occupation, government and law, consumer education, health, and community resources. The skill areas were reading, writing, computing, and problem solving. The findings for the reading segment and for overall competency, shown in Figure 1, give a good picture of the abilities of the population.

In 1979, Harmon and Hunter in *Adult Illiteracy in the U.S.: A Report to the Ford Foundation*, said that there were two levels of literacy that could be defined by a fixed inventory of skills:

1.   *Conventional literacy*--being able to read, write, and compute well enough to survive in one's environment.

2.   *Functional literacy*--(a) the possession of skills perceived by the individual to fulfil their own objectives, (b) the ability to obtain information they need or want and understand and use that information, (c) the ability to read and write adequately to satisfy themselves, (d) the ability to deal positively with the demands made by society, and (e) the ability to solve the problems they face in their daily lives.

The general goal of most literacy projects is to make individuals functionally literate.

> Over the years Jonathan Kozol, David Harman, Wally Amos, the White House, Department of Education, and others have given various definitions based on the Harman and Hunter book. Now there is a new kid on the block in the form of E. D. Hirsch, who in *Cultural Literacy: What Every American Needs to Know* (1987) says literacy is not a mechanical skill, that we need a broad base of specific information to be literate, and gives us a list of the 4,500 items that he believes an individual needs to be literate. Among them are *yuppie, Hey Diddle Diddle, Ralph Nader,* and *the id.*

Who are the illiterate? How did they get that way? There are many answers to those questions.

The stereotype often shows the illiterate as poor, out of work, and belonging to a minority group. While some illiterates have any or all of these characteristics, illiteracy affects all levels of society--no one is exempt or untouched. There are many reasons for illiteracy. some adults never went to school or may have dropped out. Many missed out in the earlier grades because they were not "ready" to learn, had poor teachers, or changed schools frequently. Others may have been affected by cultural forces such as TV or grew up in an environment where education was not valued--illiteracy breeds illiteracy. There are many more reasons--perhaps as many as there are individuals who cannot read. Whatever the reasons--illiteracy is a growing problem. It would appear that once we find a way to deal with the functionally and marginally illiterate (half of the population) we are home free--the other 46 percent are "most competent" (APL III) and are able to read well and utilize resources. True? Hardly.

Aliteracy

In 1984 D.J. Boorstin made a report to Congress called *Books in Our Future,* in which he addressed the problem of illiteracy stating very emphatically that "if people are to remain free and qualified to govern themselves we must aim to abolish illiteracy in the United States by 1989." This was a very well meaning thought but not very realistic.

In addition, he developed a second theme that further complicates and creates barriers--that of *aliteracy,* which refers to a person who can read but does not or who reads only when compelled to do so.

How many people are aliterate? The 1983 Book Industry Study Group National Survey of Reading Habits surveyed 2,000 Americans and found that almost all Americans are readers. Compared with the same study conducted five years earlier, however, a smaller proportion were reading books in 1983. The number of book readers declined by 5 percent from 1978 to 1983. The number of adults who can read but do not remained constant at 44 percent.

The study also found the decline in book readership greater among certain subgroups:

- Young adults between 16 and 20 years old fell from 75 percent to 62 percent.

- Older adults between 50 and 64 years old fell from 48 percent to 38 percent.

- Blue collar workers fell from 50 percent to 35 percent.

It is not clear whether this decline contributes to the problem of illiteracy. Literacy skills are not static. Individuals do not achieve levels of ability and stay there. Reading ability can improve or deteriorate. As with any other skill, it takes practice.

If this decline continues, aliteracy will cause a decline in the number of those who are most competent and increase the number of those who are marginally competent.

The Solution

It has been mentioned that the problem of access to information identified during this conference could be solved by "vision." Those of us who work in the literacy field have a *vision*. We believe that literacy is a basic human right and that it is up to society to devise a way for that right to be exercised. A viable approach towards a solution is one that contains the following elements: pluralistic, multilevel community based approaches and initiatives that serve the hard core disadvantaged; a major shift in national educational policy; a comprehensive design to which illiterate adults themselves contribute; and the interaction of the community with the institutions of the dominant culture. Libraries have no choice but to participate in this solution. They exist for the purpose of providing access to information and education. You are aware of the barriers. I ask you to do two things: keep in mind the barriers faced by the user whose skills are limited or nonexistent so that technology does not continue to widen the gap between the haves and have nots, and join with others and use your expertise and knowledge to help solve this problem. Help us give each individual access to the opportunity to be independent and in control of his or her own life.

For Further Reading

Boorstin, Daniel J. *Books in Our Future*, a report to Congress, 1984, and supplement *Books in Our Future: Perspectives and Proposals*. Library of Congress, Supplement, 1987.

Gann, Daniel H. "The Lifelong Learning Movement and the Role of Libraries in the Past Decade: A Bibliographic Guide." *Public Libraries* 24, no. 1 (Spring 1985).

Gross, Ronald. *Invitation to Lifelong Learning*. Follett, 1982.

Harman, David, and Hunter, Carman St. John. *Adult Illiteracy in the United States*. McGraw-Hill Book Co., 1979.

Heiser, Jane C. "Libraries, Literacy and Lifelong Learning: The Reference Connection" in *Reference Services Today: From Interview to Burnout*, Bill Katz and Ruth Fraley, eds. Haworth Press, 1987.

Heiser, Jane C. "The Public Library in the Coalition Against Illiteracy." *Public Libraries* 23, no. 4 (Winter 1984).

Johnson, Deborah, Robbins, Jane, and Zweizig. *Libraries and Literacy Education: Comprehensive Survey Report*. School of Library and Information Studies, University of Wisconsin--Madison, May 1988.

Kidd, J. R. *How Adults Learn*. Follett Publishing Co., 1973.

"Literacy," "Libraries and Literacy." *ALA Yearbook*, 1977-current.

Lyman, Helen Huguenor. *Literacy and the Nations Libraries*. American Library Association, 1977.

Lyman, Helen Huguenor. *Reading and the Adult New Reader*. American Library Association, 1976.

A Resource Guide to United States Government Publications About Literacy. Washington, D.C.: GPO, May 1988.

U.S. Office of Education. Final Report: *The Adult Performance Level Study*, 1977.

U.S. Department of Education. Office of Libraries and Learning Technologies. *Libraries in Literacy*, 1981.

Technologies and Barriers to Information Access

S. MICHAEL MALINCONICO

School of Computer, Information and Library Sciences
Pratt Institute
Brooklyn, N.Y.

Although libraries make the problem of gaining access to information manageable, they are unquestionably complicated and difficult to use. As a matter of economic exigency they are generally self-service facilities. Even the best organized and best run libraries present a variety of barriers to their users. In what follows we will discuss three common barriers and the extent to which modern technologies have lowered them, raised them, or created new ones. First, we will consider physical barriers, that is, obstacles impeding physical access to the materials that libraries collect. Then we will take up conceptual barriers, that is, problems arising from the nature of the tools that are available to a library's users to facilitate their use of its collections. And finally, we will examine fiscal barriers, that is, difficulties created by the scarcity of the resources needed to provide adequate service.

We should note at the outset, however, that our everyday experiences with the products of modern technologies have served to raise our expectations. We expect the organizations we deal with to supply us with detailed information immediately, regardless where that information is maintained. We are no longer willing to tolerate delays while a particular problem is researched and we expect to receive services at the place and time of our choosing. For example, a person with a question about a charge on a bill expects to obtain immediate detailed information about it while he or she is on the telephone; a traveler in Chicago expects to know immediately, not in several days or hours, whether space is available on a flight from Paris to Rome; or a bank customer, even if his or her account is with a bank on the other side of town, expects to be able to withdraw money regardless of banking hours. Likewise, it is insufficient to speak of barriers to access to a library's holdings, but rather we need to consider barriers to the satisfaction of a user's information needs, independent of the resources of any particular library. This at once expands the possibilities for satisfying a user's needs and makes the problem of gaining access to specific materials more complex.

Physical Barriers

First, we will consider space, or distance, as a barrier, as technology has very effectively dealt with this problem without introducing any significant new problems to take its place.

The information libraries have traditionally collected is of a specific kind. It is generally recorded on some physical medium, which is maintained or stored in some specific place. Until very recently, one could only consult that information by gaining physical access to the objects on which it is recorded. Space, or distance, can present a truly formidable barrier to access.

Reduction by Technology

Libraries have long recognized this problem as well as the related problem of being unable to acquire and maintain sufficiently comprehensive collections to satisfy all of the needs of all their users. The obvious solution to this problem is embodied in the interlibrary loan networks that have been developed and flourish in this country and that are steadily being extended to encompass the entire world. ILL systems have always been heavily dependent on innovative uses of communication technologies, for example, teletypes have long been used to communicate ILL requests rapidly to resource libraries and the punched paper tape that they generate is frequently used to forward requests to other sources when a library cannot fill a request. More recently support of interlibrary loan activity has become one of the most important products of the massive, computerized databases the bibliographic utilities have been amassing.

We can expect that in the relatively near future most libraries will have their own local systems to control their collections, and that computer-to-computer and communications standards, which will permit users of one local systems to interrogate a remote system to determine the present availability of materials, will be developed, and generally adopted. Library users can have highly convenient access to the materials held by their local libraries and with little more difficulty access to materials contained in cooperating, remote collections.

Online union catalogs help to penetrate the walls that separate cooperating library systems and eliminate, or at least reduce, the barriers that physical separation would impose among cooperating libraries.

This is a particularly good example of the unqualified success that modern technologies have had in reducing barriers to information access. We can look forward to the steady improvement of these capabilities.

I would now like to turn to less clear-cut examples: the conceptual barriers created by the nature of our bibliographic tools.

Conceptual Barriers

Complexity of Tools

Libraries do not lack for tools to facilitate access to information. They generally present to their users a bewildering array of catalogs, indexes, bibliographies, and directories. These tools are generally uncoordinated and have varying--frequently overlapping--scopes of coverage, different methods of organization, often similar, but not identical, content, dissimilar indexing terminology, and different display formats. In the hands of a skilled librarian or someone familiar with them, these tools are enormously effective in facilitating access to information. But to someone unfamiliar with their idiosyncrasies and the differences among them, they present an additional puzzle that needs to be solved. The first obstacle a user encounters is a surfeit, not an absence, of tools to facilitate access to information.

Training

In order to use a library effectively, a user needs to devote considerable effort to mastering its resources and the tools available to facilitate their use. Some heavy users of particular collections do just this, either through conscious effort or as a fortuitous consequence of repeated exposure. For most people this is generally impractical. Their use of a library's resources is not sufficiently frequent that they are able to develop the experience or familiarity necessary to make efficient, effective use of those resources. They must rely on the assistance of the public service staff.

Few libraries (other than special, or corporate, libraries) can afford to provide their users with extensive personal assistance in the use of their collections. Even if they could, such assistance might not prove very useful in most instances. Users are frequently unable at the outset to describe clearly what their information needs are. The objects of their information needs emerge clearly only in the course of searching for appropriate material. In order to get the help they need, they would need to be in relatively constant dialog with librarians who are both conversant with the subject matter they are researching and familiar with the information sources that exist on that subject. This is clearly impractical. Lack of adequate access to professional staff is an important barrier that impedes access to information.

Format of Tools

Once a user has overcome the initial hurdle of selecting the right tools, he or she must contend with the problems posed by the physical and organizational format of those tools. Most bibliographic tools are in the form of printed volumes representing cumulations of information for varying periods of time or arrays of drawers of 3" x 5" cards. Since these tools are language-based, users must first solve the problem of recasting their information needs into the language, or terminology, employed by those tools. This often includes following a chain of references from headings in one part of the alphabet to another. The problems of physical access are compounded when users need to consult multiple cumulations or multiple sources simultaneously.

As any user of indexing tools knows, having located a citation to a promising source is only part of the battle. The next and more important step is determining whether the particular monograph, report, or issue of a periodical cited is held by the library and whether it is currently available. This usually requires that the library's catalogs or serial record be consulted.

The display formats employed in many bibliographic tools create other barriers to ready access to information. Card catalogs have traditionally been created from unit cards that are duplicated and filed under multiple headings. In the interests of economy the same unit record serve the needs of many different users: casual users of a general library, the library's collection development and acquisitions staff, and serious researchers. The same card that is filed into a library's public catalog is also filed into its official catalog as an official, authoritative bibliographic record and into its shelflist as an official inventory record. The records found in card catalogs are generally designed to serve the needs of a library's most sophisticated users, and since these cards are usually the product of national programs, they are designed to serve the needs of the most sophisticated users of the most sophisticated libraries. As a result, they frequently contain a great deal of information that is superfluous, or just plain distracting, to many people.

On the other hand, in order to keep the size of card files and printed catalogs, or bibliographies, manageable, it is necessary to abbreviate as much as possible the entries they contain. The result is usually entries that contain a great deal of information that is cryptic to all but a small minority of users and that largely serves to obscure the information that is of primary interest to most users. Requiring that users master tools too refined for their purposes creates serious impediments to their ability to use a library.[1]

Indexing Terminology

Finally, printed indexes can only anticipate the questions that will be put to them, so their organization often fails to provide ready access to the specific information sought by specific users. Although most indexes, directories, and catalogs provide multiple access points, the number of access points is necessarily limited by the nature of the physical media in which they are produced. An item that deals with various aspects of a subject is usually listed only under a limited number of those access characteristics. Similarly, an item that deals with a highly specific combination of access characteristics is commonly listed under each of these separately. In general, users find grouped under an appropriate head a relatively limited collection of items that they must scan to find those that satisfy their specific information needs. When the object of one's search is relatively complex, this can be a tedious and unreliable undertaking.

Library users have a substantial number of obstacles to overcome before they can even get to examine materials in order to make a final determination of their usefulness. These barriers are created by the nature of the access tools available to them.

Reduction by Technology

Let us consider how technology has, or might, reduce these barriers:

Online, Interactive Systems

Computer technologies seem to have solved fairly well some of the problems noted in the foregoing--those created by distance, physical format, and static indexing terminology. Online, interactive systems permit users to access a comprehensive collection of information conveniently from a single location. There is rarely a need to distinguish among data added to a database at different times. When one searches a computerized database, that search is generally conducted against the entire file. Nonetheless, most online database systems permit searches to be restricted by period, if that proves convenient. (It should be noted that some online databases have grown so large that they too have been divided chronologically. But this is the exception rather than the rule, and it does not appear to be an obstacle that is difficult to overcome.)

Likewise, following a chain of references with an online system is generally a relatively simple matter of entering a few keystrokes. Many online systems provide the capability to "expand" a search term to display related terms, including accepted and unaccepted synonyms, narrower terms, and broader terms. Computerized display technologies generally impose few practical limitations on the number of access points a record may have. All of the combinations and permutations of the indexing terms assigned to records in a database are potential access terms. These terms are not combined until a search query is formulated, so materials that satisfy a number of conditions or that share any indexed attribute in common can be readily accessed. For example, one could retrieve all materials dealing with the use of teaching machines in English speaking countries, select all materials dealing with education in the English speaking Caribbean, select all materials on Antigua, or select all materials on teaching machines regardless of where they are used. With traditional, static sources a user would have needed to consult one or several sequences and select from them the items that appeared to be relevant.

Computerized displays can be adapted to a variety of circumstances and can be put under the control of the individuals using them. The display of the same record presented to a cataloger or bibliographer can be quite different from that presented to a casual user, or the information presented to a single user could be quite different depending on circumstances. For example, when a user is engaged in a browsing activity, only the briefest and most essential elements need be presented to him or her, yet he or she should retain the ability to select an individual record for closer examination. This could be under manual control. A fully developed system, however, would "know" when a user is engaged in a browsing activity and automatically default to a brief format to facilitate scanning large numbers of records, and would switch to a fuller format when a user has identified a specific record. In addition, if a library chooses, abbreviations could be expanded, cryptic punctuation eliminated and each of the elements of a complex record labeled. Many of the currently available online catalogs provide at least some of these options. Technology has been relatively successful in eliminating the manner in which information is indexed, organized, and presented to users as barriers.

Online Bibliographic Instruction

As appealing as online catalogs with sophisticated Boolean capabilities may be, greater advantage will be found in the ability of online, interactive systems to guide and coach their users. The personal computer industry has changed our conception of what is an appropriate balance of effort in a person machine interaction, and changed our expectations of the way computer programs are supposed to interact with their users. When personal computers were a novelty, producers of microcomputer software had the formidable challenge of selling software to people who had little technical knowledge and equally little incentive to spend large amounts of time mastering a new tool that was supposed to save them time and effort. Those vendors markedly changed the focus of software design and development. Previously the focus had been on what software did--on its power and sophistication--rather than on how it performed its functions. It was expected that computer users possessed sufficient technical sophistication to adapt to the idiosyncrasies of software systems and that the benefits to be gained from the software justified the effort needed to learn to use it.

The nature of the personal computer industry shifted the focus from technology to the user. Software vendors devoted unprecedented attention to the user interface. They produced systems that were as intuitively obvious to operate as possible. In many cases, they incorporated user manuals into the systems themselves. They allocated some fraction of the computer's processing capability and internal memory to keeping track of where users are and what they are trying to do, so that they can get highly specific, context-sensitive help should they need it.

Similar features are beginning to appear in online library systems. Online catalogs have the capability of being not just a convenient way to access information that describes a library's holdings, they can also serve as platforms for computer-assisted bibliographic instruction. Clearly, we have the ability to design systems that can assist people not only in using software packages, or online public access catalogs, but that can provide help tailored to the individual's needs from a library and its resources. As the capabilities of expert systems become more accessible, we will increasingly find the expertise of skilled librarians incorporated into automated systems. This, not the development of yet another online system with interactive search capability, will be a truly significant breakthrough, as it will address the most fundamental barrier to gaining access to information: the need for expert assistance in using a library, its collections, and its access tools.

Remote Assistance

Communication technologies permit information services to be delivered to remote locations. This is true whether the service is an answer to a question provided by a telephone reference service, a response to an online catalog query, or a bibliographic citation retrieved from an online database. Recent developments in data communication and VDT technologies allow computer terminals to display both digital information retrieved from computerized databases and video images. For example, DataPoint markets terminals with built-in video cameras that can exchange full motion video with similar terminals operating on a local area network and can be switched to receive and display digital information retrieved from databases accessible through the same local area network.

Such a capability presents enormous opportunities to establish ultra-sophisticated facilities that can help people use online systems, complement the services available from computerized systems, or provide the means to multiply the accessibility of skilled public service staff. For example, in late 1987 the California State University at Long Beach installed a pilot DataPoint system employing three video terminals. In principle a reference librarian located at any of those terminals is simultaneously accessible to students at three different locations. In a sense, the effective value of that reference librarian is tripled. These systems are still relatively expensive. The list price of the Long Beach system is approximately $35,900, exclusive of wiring. Nonetheless, assuming an annual salary of $25,000 and fringes of 30 percent for a reference librarian, and even assuming conservatively high operating costs of $10,000 per year for the video system, one could still amortize the cost of such a system in less than two years.

Of course the arithmetic presented here is somewhat ingenuous, as the library might not have planned to put reference librarians at two additional locations, so there might not be a reduction in personnel costs that could be used to pay for the system. Nonetheless, by any reasonable measure, the library is able to deliver more service, and whatever barriers to access to a professional librarian students might have encountered are substantially lowered.

System Integration

Finally, increased system integration will address the impediments created by the need for users to access a number of independent files or system facilities in order to satisfy their information needs. For example, after a user has consulted an online database and retrieved a number of promising citations, his or her next question would be, "are the journals, reports, and monographs cited in the database response held by the library?" This might require access to the library's catalog, serials control file, or some other less formal control record.

If the items cited are articles in periodicals, one would want to know not just whether the library subscribes to those journals, but whether the particular issues cited have been received and are currently available. This would probably require access to a library's serial records. If the items cited are monographs, one would want to know whether they are currently available; if not, one might wish to place a reserve for them, or, if possible, request that they be recalled. This would require access to a library's online circulation system. Finally, if some of the items sought are not available in the library, one might wish to know whether they are held by institutions with which the library has interlibrary lending or reciprocal use arrangements. This would require access to the library's cooperative, resource sharing system, that is, online union catalog, or shared cataloging system.

At present there is no system that allows all of the foregoing activity to be negotiated at a single workstation. Nonetheless, such a facility would be highly desirable. Before we can achieve this, we must await the development of a truly comprehensive integrated system. I think, however, that this is unlikely, and is an impractical goal. It might be more realistic and advantageous to work toward the development of standards to ensure open systems interconnection, that is, standard interfaces among individual systems that will permit a comprehensive, integrated system to be realized by interconnecting several limited purpose system components.

The development of these standards, their adoption by vendors, and their incorporation by vendors into their products will provide the structures needed to configure a variety of powerful new tools that will put users in total command of a library's information resources.

This, I think, is the principal technical challenge of the remainder of the century. It is an outcome anxiously awaited by many of the largest users of computer technology--not just libraries--so we can remain sanguine that it will come to pass in the next ten to fifteen years, that is, before the end of the century.

New Barriers to Be Surmounted

The Need for Computer Literacy

There is little question that modern information handling technologies can and will improve access to information. For at least the foreseeable future, however, the use of these systems will be unnatural and alien to most people. In order for users to realize the benefits we have described, they will need to possess a level of ease with machines and computer literacy that many of them do not possess.

The first impediment many users encounter is the need to use a keyboard. Because most people are unfamiliar with the layout of a keyboard, they find using one is a frustrating, time consuming process of hunting and pecking for elusive letters and special keys. Even people who are relatively good typists find keyboards a frustratingly slow way to communicate with an information system. The frustration of using a keyboard is aggravated by the need to remember often cryptic commands and their syntax, and the need to spell correctly the terms that describe the information one is seeking. Turning the pages of a book or flipping through index cards are far more intuitively obvious actions than entering commands to retrieve data, to display the next screen, the previous screen, or the "sixth screen after the next."

These barriers may be of long term significance. It seems unlikely that the educational system will produce a computer literate society in the foreseeable future. By the end of the century those people who are now 18 years of age or older (i.e., those who have already left high school) will make up nearly 60 percent of the population.[2] They will probably not be much more computer literate--or for that matter print literate--than they are now. So it seems highly likely that the capabilities of technology will advance far more rapidly than the ability of most people to utilize it.

Nonetheless, there will be a variety of other solutions to this problem, some of which are already in evidence. They will include the use of menus, pointing devices (such as mice), touch screens, keyboards or keypads with special purpose keys instead of normal typewriter keys, programmable function keys whose functions are indicated as prompts on the video display, the use of icons in place of text to represent menu choices, and further progress on voice input.

Computer processes are rigorously logical and consistent, nonetheless, they usually manage to surprise most people. Few people are prepared to deal with the frustratingly literal logic of a computer that always seems to retrieve either too many items, too few items, or none. There is little in the ordinary experience of most people that teaches them how to recast a query in terms that are more restrictive or less restrictive depending on circumstances. Constructing appropriate qualifiers that reduce a response containing an unmanageable number of entries or expand the scope of a search argument sufficiently to yield usable results requires ingenuity and mental agility few people have much occasion to exercise and perfect.

The introduction of complex, new systems into libraries will have many unanticipated consequences. For example, the relative complexity of these facilities may create what Sanford Berman has termed, "'librarian-dependence' (i.e., undue reliance upon 'professionals' as information intermediaries)."[3] This will doubtless do much to enhance the status of librarians, but may also contribute to feelings of inadequacy among users and potential users reinforcing and raising barriers to library use.

Sophisticated information access tools lower barriers for those who learn to use them, but raise new barriers for those who have difficulty learning to do so. Traditional bibliographic access tools--card catalogs, printed indexes, and so forth although inefficient, cumbersome, and unresponsive in some cases, can, at least, be used by anyone; this may not be so for the newer electronic technologies. As electronic tools replace traditional ones, barriers will be lowered for many, but for others, newer, perhaps more formidable barriers will be erected.

Displays

Computerized database systems can retrieve individual records that satisfy the most complex criteria from among many hundreds of thousands of other records. They can also retrieve many hundreds of unwanted records in response to imprecisely formulated search criteria. A typical display presents fewer than twenty-five lines of eighty characters each, so reviewing a lengthy list of responses on a VDT screen can be quite tedious. It is not possible to view and compare widely separated entries. One does not have the luxury of using slips of paper, or even his or her fingers, to mark multiple places in printed volumes or various cards in a card catalog.

The limited scope of VDT displays militates against finding information by serendipity. The restricted number of entries presented to view at any given time aggravates problems created by data input errors. Even the smallest error in a data element that determines the position of an entry on a VDT screen may put that entry out of the range of view. Admittedly, the same problem exists with card files. Trivial errors are as likely to go unnoticed by card filers and end users as by the person who made the error. Computers are not so tolerant.

These are perhaps problems of the moment, which we can expect more developed software and better displays to remedy. There is already noticeable progress in this regard. Several years ago IBM introduced a plasma display terminal whose screen is divided into four quadrants each of which is a full twenty-five-line x eighty-character display; several vendors have already introduced various kinds of "windowing" software; and some online public access catalogs allow users to save individual entries in a notepad area for later review.

Multiple Access Protocols

Many libraries now employ, or have access to, a variety of automated systems. Users frequently need access to several of these systems to complete a search for information. Most of these systems, which have been developed independently of each other, employ unique access protocols and present different interfaces to users, posing a formidable problem to the casual or uninitiated user. It will very likely be a long time before user interfaces are sufficiently standard or simple to overcome this problem. Nonetheless, notable progress has already been made. Committee G of the United States National Information Standards Organization (NISO) has been working to develop a standard for a common command language. In March 1986 the proposed standard was circulated to NISO's voting members for review and comment. The purpose of the committee's draft standard is to specify the vocabulary, syntax, and operational meaning of commands in a command language for use with on-line interactive retrieval systems. When the standard is adopted by NISO, it is anticipated that many on-line search systems that employ a command language will either adopt the standard commands as a native language or support them as a search option.[4]

Fiscal Barriers

I would like to turn to issues of cost and fiscal barriers. Clearly, modern technologies have been instrumental in controlling the rate of rise of costs in libraries. It is not clear whether they have saved great amounts of money, but they have unquestionably made technical services operations more productive and in general contributed to improving the quality of a variety of activities.

Online shared cataloging systems and union catalogs have permitted some libraries to reallocate funds that would have otherwise been spent to acquire and process costly, arcane, or little used materials. These funds are often used for more copies of in-demand materials, a greater selection of these materials or for more public service staff.

Substantial costs are usually associated with the new electronic technologies. Libraries wishing to employ them must find the money to pay for them. The most likely assumption is that for the foreseeable future there will not be any substantial new funding available to pay for new library services; so in order to pay for new electronic systems, the resources allocated to other, existing services must be reduced. There is insufficient evidence to demonstrate that automated systems displace sufficient costs to pay for themselves. In fact, the opposite seems to be the case--costs often increase. This equation is much too ingenuous to be useful as a means for judging allocation priorities, as automated systems frequently provide the capability to deliver more units of service, to do things that were either long neglected as a consequence of economic exigency, or to do things that are desirable, but impractical in a manual environment. Nonetheless, as a simple quantitative statement it is true, which inexorably leads to the conclusion that the implementation of automated systems must be supported by the reallocation of available resources.

Although there are systems that improve services for all of a library's users, such as automated circulation systems, existing high technology systems tend to cater to a library's most sophisticated users. The best developed systems are those that facilitate access to business-related information and esoteric scholarly information in disciplines that already enjoy superior funding. This is a simple reflection of economic reality, not a qualitative assessment of the importance of this kind of information. Convenient, timely access to business information in a form that permits it to be easily analyzed can be directly related to economic advantage. As a result, individuals and organizations are willing to pay handsomely for it. It is not surprising that such information sources are abundantly available.

Such a ready equation cannot be established for the value of information useful to people in the conduct of their daily lives, for example, directories of community social service agencies; databases of employment opportunities with interactive capability to match an individual's skills, abilities, and employment objectives and job openings; databases that can assist individuals in locating the appropriate official agency or public official to deal with a problem; or databases of educational opportunities with interactive ability to match individuals and specific educational programs; or databases of consumer information.

If resources are reallocated to pay for advanced technologies, it is likely that business, science, and technology-related information will be favored at the expense of other kinds of library services, such as services to children and young adults, recreational and cultural services, and self-improvement services.

Even if the new electronic services can be supported by reallocating only resources normally budgeted for business, science, and technology-related acquisitions, there would still be forces that might prevent conventional services from receiving equitable support. The new technology-based services will require special skills. Librarians involved with them will have greater opportunities to display their professional abilities. They will be on a faster track. The result will be that these services will attract the best and most qualified individuals, leaving shortages in other branches of library service.

Finally, we might also note that online services, being the most glamorous, will tend to claim greater amounts of the time of individual librarians, again, possibly to the detriment of other services.

Sophisticated online services will clearly play an important part in reducing certain barriers but will also have the potential for creating other barriers or impediments.

The situation is perhaps even more malignant than the foregoing might suggest. All libraries are affected whether they choose to employ the products of modern technology or not. As automated alternatives to conventional bibliographic tools gain acceptance, the latter will either begin to disappear, or because demand for them diminishes, will cost more. The advance of technology creates barriers for those who use libraries with relatively modest resources. It could be argued in a Darwinian sense that such libraries will be consolidated and replaced by agencies able to provide superior levels of service. This, however, ignores the difficulties that many library users might have getting to improved replacements for their local libraries: children, older adults, the mobility impaired, or those people who do not need highly specialized materials and who live in rural areas. For people who have only modest needs, technological advances will reduce few barriers and may even erect substantial new ones.

Conclusion

The jury is still out on whether modern technologies will lower barriers to information access. We know of numerous barriers that have been lowered, and we know of many more that creative implementation of these technologies will lower or eliminate in the relatively near future, but we also know of some new ones that will be introduced. These new barriers appear to be particularly troubling, as they have the potential to disenfranchise substantial segments of the population--those who are the most vulnerable: the least educated, the least affluent, and those who have already been victimized once by technologies that displaced them from the workforce.

Notes

1. Sanford Berman, *HCL Cataloging Bulletin,* no. 32 (January/February 1978), Added entries: The cataloging mystique--and automation, 15-22.

2. *Statistical Abstract of the United States,* 107th ed., Washington, D.C.: U.S. Government Printing Office, 1986, Tables 13 and 16.

3. Sanford Berman, 1. Libraries--Forecasts. 2. Elitism in Librarianship, *Library Journal* 105 (1 January 1980):23-27.

4. Charles R. Hildreth, The U.S. National Standard Command Language for Online Interactive Information Retrieval: A Status Report, Proceedings, Symposium on Impact of New Information Technology on International Library Cooperation, Essen, 8-11 September 1986, ed. Ahmed H. Helal and Joachim W. Weiss, Essen University Library, 1987, 73-84.

Bibliography

Bekiares, Susan E. "Technology for the Handicapped: Selection and Evaluation of Aids and Devices for the Visually Impaired." *Library Hi Tech* 2 (1984):57-61.

Berman, Sanford. *HCL Cataloging Bulletin,* no. 32 (January/February 1978). Added entries: The cataloging mystique--and automation, 15-22.

_____. "1. Libraries--Forecasts. 2. Elitism in Librarianship," *Library Journal* 105 (1 January 1980):23-27.

_____. "Predictions." In *Beyond "1984": The Future of Library Technical Services*. Edited by Peter Gellatly. New York: The Haworth Press, 1983, 61-63.

Cochrane, Pauline A. "Can a Standard for an Online Common Command Language Be Developed?" *Online* 7 (January 1983):36-37.

Cotter, Eithne, and McCarty, Emily. "Technology for the Handicapped: Kurzweil and Viewscan." *Library Hi Tech* 1 (Winter 1983):63-67.

Demas, Samuel G. "Freedom of Access to Information in Machine Readable Form: The Librarian's Role." In Association of College and Research Libraries, National Conference, (4th: 1986: Baltimore, Md.), Energies for Transition, Proceedings, Association of College & Research Libraries, 1986.

Hildreth, Charles R. The U.S. National Standard Command Language for Online Interactive Information Retrieval: A Status Report, Proceedings, Symposium on Impact of New Information Technology on International Library Cooperation, Essen, 8-11 September 1986. Edited by Ahmed H. Helal and Joachim W. Weiss. Essen University Library, 1987, 73-84.

Konoshima, Sumiye. "Barriers and Prospects for Transborder Data Flow." *Bulletin of the American Society for Information Science* 13 (April/May 1987):32-33.

Lipetz, Ben-Ami. "Catalog Use in a Large Research Library." *Library Quarterly* 42 (January 1972):129-39.

Markey, Karen. "Barriers to Effective Use of Online Catalogs." In *Online Catalogs, Online Reference.* Chicago: American Library Association, 1984.

Potter, William Gary. "Libraries, Computing Centers, and Freedom of Access." *Journal of Academic Librarianship* 13 (libraries and computing centers, issue no. 5):298.

Redfern, Brian. "Dinosaurs to Crush Flies: Computer Catalogues, Classification and Other Barriers to Library Use." *Brio* 21 (Spring/Summer 1984):4-8.

Seff, Laura. "The Public Library Search Helper: Going Online Easily and Economically." *Small Computers in Libraries* 6 (October 1986):29-32.

Toliver, David E. "OL'SAM: An Intelligent Front-end for Bibliographic Information Retrieval." *Information Technology and Libraries* 1 (December 1982):317-26.

United States Congress, Joint Committee on Printing, Ad Hoc Committee on Depository Library Access to Federal Automated Data Bases. *Provision of Federal Government Publications in Electronic Format to Depository Libraries.* Washington, D.C.: United States Government Printing Office, 1984.

White, Herbert S. "The Other Barriers to Information Access." *Library Journal* 111 (15 November 1986):60-61.

Staff Attitudes: Conflicting Values

LEIGH STEWART ESTABROOK

Dean, Graduate School of Library and Information Science
University of Illinois at Urbana-Champaign
Urbana, Illinois

The original title of this paper, as assigned by Al Trezza, was "Staff Attitudes: A Basic Ingredient." As I considered that statement, it seemed there was a perfect solution to being the last speaker on the last day of this intense conference. I could stand up and say, "You are absolutely right, staff attitudes are the basic ingredient," and then I could sit down--brief, to the point, no unnecessary verbiage. One problem for me in doing this is that for over a decade I have had a nagging concern with the question, if staff attitudes are, in fact, assumed by us to be the critical ingredient, why do we have such difficulty in our professional practice? If, as I believe, there is a shared commitment by librarians to making information accessible, why are there problems in achieving the goals of accessibility? I will try to consider conflicting values in library practice that create those barriers to access about which we are concerned.

I would like to begin with a discussion of three different ways in which conflicting values enter into the play of professional practice and professional attitudes. After that I will discuss several points in a recent work in moral philosophy that I believe give some insight into our struggle. I will conclude with what I take to be the implication of that philosophical analysis for our professional practice.

Summary of the Argument

Let me begin by summarizing the three apparent contradictions.

Contradiction 1: Libraries that have a mission to serve all their public provide unequal access in their hierarchies of service.

Evidence: In an article written ten years ago[1] I noted that services to a library's general public were often sacrificed for services to some of the elite sectors of the community (e.g., businesspeople, faculty). I would argue the trend is even stronger today and would point to evidence presented by Malinconico in his paper for added support.

Explanation: When resources are scarce and choices for services must be made, it often seems necessary to retain those services valued by those economically and politically influential users at the expense of services targeted toward less powerful groups. The formal goals of the institution are replaced by its instrumental goals of survival and fund raising.

Contradiction 2: Despite professional commitment to equality of access, libraries frequently prefer to serve more elite, better educated clients.

Evidence: Margaret Kimmel in her dissertation[2] studied librarians' attitudes toward clients and found them to be ambivalent and contradictory. Her data further suggest "that librarians associate socio-economic status of the client with how well the service will or will not be received."[3] Again, I would point to Malinconico's recent example of "fast track" librarians and their vision of online services as glamorous.

Explanation: Kimmel found librarians to be similar to other "striving" occupations. "The more public librarians were concerned about the status and image of the group, the less likely it was that the respondents would have a high regard for lower class clients."[4] Sociologists of occupations have often noted that the status of a profession and even of an individual within a profession is correlated with the clients being served: physicians with higher status, for example, are those who treat adults or work in communities with higher class clients. Pediatricians and physicians in city hospitals do not garner the same respect as those in private practice in wealthy communities. Given the concern of librarians with increasing the status of librarianship, it is not surprising that the phenomenon exists. (I should note that striving for status is not solely a negative phenomenon. Higher status of the profession may correlate well with librarians holding greater weight in political and economic decisions about access to information.)

Contradiction 3: If librarianship is committed to access, how can it embrace information resources management (IRM), the primary purpose of which is efficient and effective use of information in economic terms.

Evidence: As I noted in a recent article[5] and as we see in the presentations at this conference, there is a convergence of librarianship and information resources management. The practice of librarianship (which includes acquisition, organization, and dissemination of information) is expanding its institutional boundaries and linking with that practice concerned with the efficient and effective management of information. Efficiency and effectiveness, however, do not always lead to maximum accessibility. Economic models that dominate analyses of cost effective ways to manage information often lead to the conclusion that limiting access (by the types of materials acquired or the fees charged for use) is the most rational approach to information management.

Explanation: The United States economy is based on increasingly narrow definitions of public goods and what should be supported by public funds. And those services that are publicly supported are expected to run more "profitably." Libraries are part of that society and are reminded repeatedly that it is not possible to do everything for free. In the absence of widely accepted economic models of how to measure the benefits to society of wide access to information resources, librarians are forced into using those models understood by their governing bodies and their public.

We can reduce the explanation for each of these three contradictory problems to a concern for the survival of libraries as institutions and librarianship as a profession. Without the external goals of power, prestige, and resources, it is argued, those two institutions (libraries and the profession of librarianship) will lose out to the competition from the information industry and the other information professions.

Perhaps so, but let me argue in response that unless we find some way to hold on to what is intrinsically contained in the practice of librarianship--namely the commitment to access--then we will lose our identity anyway.

In struggling to understand this dilemma, I have come to believe that the problem we confront in "staff attitudes" is as much a moral and philosophical problem as a question of the particular competence each of us brings our work as librarians. And in trying to shape a response to this dilemma, I have gained much insight from Alasdair MacIntyre's important book, *After Virtue.*[6]

MacIntyre is concerned with "practice" and what he calls "the internal goods of practice." MacIntyre states that a practice "is never just a set of technical skills, even when directed toward some unified purpose and even if the exercise of those skills can on occasion be valued or enjoyed for their own sake. What is distinctive in a practice is in part the way in which conceptions of the relevant goods and ends that the technical skills serve--and every practice does require the exercise of technical skills--are transformed and enriched by these extensions of human power and by that regard for its own internal goods, which are partially definitive of each particular practice or type of practice."[7]

This ethical notion of "internal goods" of practice is one that I believe most librarians understand. The profession of librarianship is more than the exercise of technical skills. The practice of the profession involves the application of skills and knowledge to specific ends. Acquiring materials or organizing them for use has no meaning without reference to the purposes of that acquiring and organizing. One of our overriding ends for doing such work is to make materials accessible to those who need and can use them.

Within librarianship, the foundation of practice--extending access to information--is clearly one of the internal goods of practice--it is related to the notion of "doing librarianship in its most complete form."

MacIntyre views internal goods of practice in the context of human virtue. He postulates that "A virtue is an acquired human quality the possession and exercise of which tends to enable us to achieve those goods that are internal to practices and the lack of which effectively prevents us from achieving any such goods."[8] He goes on to argue that "we have to accept as necessary components of any practice with internal goods and standards of excellence the virtues of justice, courage and honesty."[9]

The logical connection between MacIntyre's notion of virtue and the "virtue" of providing equality of access to materials in the practice of librarianship can be seen if we examine his statement on justice. "Justice," MacIntyre notes, "requires that we treat others . . . according to uniform and impersonal standards; to depart from the standards of justice in some particular instance defines our relationship with the relevant person as in some way special or distinctive."[10] Justice in our practice would seem to mean that we treat all users equitably without regard for such attributes as social status, level of education, or ability to pay.

I recognize that subjecting librarianship to the test of moral philosophy may seem foreign and somewhat disturbing. But on what other grounds do we as librarians argue for providing equal access to materials other than on the grounds that to do so is just. If we can accept the existence of this moral base to librarianship, it is logical to ask next why the contradictions cited above exist.

McIntyre is talking about individual virtues--not the virtue of a profession nor of a library. This is a crucial distinction. People are virtuous. There is no meaningful way in which institutions can be. And it is here that the source of contradiction lies.

Practices must not be confused with institutions. Chess, physics, and medicine are practices; chess clubs, laboratories, universities, and hospitals are institutions. Institutions are characteristically and necessarily concerned with what I have called external goods. They are involved in acquiring money and other material goods, they are structured in terms of power and status, and they distribute money, power, and status as rewards. Nor could they do otherwise if they are to sustain not only themselves, but also the practices of which they are the bearers. For no practices can survive for any length of time unsustained by institutions. Indeed so intimate is the relationship of practices to institutions that institutions and practices characteristically form a single causal order in which the ideals and the creativity of practice are always vulnerable to the acquisitiveness of the institution, in which the cooperative care for common goods of the practice is always vulnerable to the competitiveness of the institution.[11]

We can relate this statement to libraries if we think about three "actors" in librarianship: (1) the library as an institution, (2) librarianship as a profession and (3) the library professional. The first exists as a concrete entity--by itself and linked with other libraries, with the information industry, with users, and with groups of users. As noted earlier, in order to survive libraries must compete effectively, they must strive for resources, and recognition. While accessibility may be a primary institutional goal, it is one that will be compromised-traded off--balanced out--as libraries seek to achieve institutional viability.

The second component, the profession of librarianship, can also be understood institutionally. As a group, librarians strive to enhance their prestige, access to resources, and other external goods. It is a legitimate concern of the profession to seek to obtain societal recognition and societal rewards for the work of its members. In the process, there are also bound to be compromises of the sort noted above.

As I think MacIntyre's quote makes clear, the fact that such compromises are made does not make libraries or the library profession "bad." The trade-offs regarding access to materials that these two groups make must be evaluated in light of their instrumental goals of survival and institutional growth. Institutions and professions have missions. They have goals. They do not have values. People have values. It is the individual who must resist the corrupting power of even the most noble institutions. It is only individuals who can behave courageously or with justice.

We are led then to some inevitable conclusions about staff attitudes and information access. First, we must accept as natural and ongoing the tension (even conflict) between how we practice librarianship and how we meet our institutional obligations. If we are to act with integrity as individuals, we can expect to find ourselves constantly challenging the institutions in which we practice.

This is obviously difficult. Many of us wear three hats: we are professionals in practice as individuals, we are professionals involved in the growth of the profession, and we are managers responsible for the viability and vitality of the institutions that employ us. There may in fact be circumstances in which we can only act with virtue by setting ourselves apart from our institutions and resigning or acting in such a way in which we are asked to resign.

Confronting this inherent schizophrenia of our practice as librarians is at once terrifying and liberating. Terrifying because taking a position against that of an inherently more powerful institution is difficult. It is even more so when one's career and livelihood are intimately bound up with that institution. At the same time it is liberating to recognize the inevitability of the struggle between the institution and individual--to recognize that one's own disagreements are not simply a personal aberration but born of the essential commitment that is made when "called" to the profession of librarianship.

Although we are called upon to act individually to realize the "internal goods of practice," we do not act alone. The commitment to providing access to materials is a shared value, one held by our colleagues in the profession and one supported by the profession. The support for our behavior begins with our professional education and continues with our professional associations and our colleagues.

Many of us responsible for educating library and information science professionals recognize our obligation to educate our students "in virtue"--in the ethical and moral base of the profession. I will, however, readily admit the almost impossible task of doing so as fully as we might like. With the diverse backgrounds of our students, we can become so caught up in giving students the necessary skills of practice that it is difficult to set aside sufficient time to talk about the ethics of how those skills are used. Most of our programs are one year long. Even those that extend two years are filled with "technical" courses. As I review curricula from the Illinois program and from others, it is obvious that we work in this direction--in our discussions of intellectual freedom, in our work on the reference interview and question negotiation, and in our presentations on the principals of cataloging and classification, to name just a few. Perhaps the increased emphasis on ethics in the education of business school students will give ethical education the academic status it needs to be seen as more acceptable in all curricula.

The profession also provides support for the virtues of practice through such activities as the ALA Washington Office's "Less Access to More Information . . ." publication or association condemnation of the Library Awareness Program. Individual librarians involved in censorship efforts also may be assisted by professional solidarity. As I noted above, however, institutional support is bound to be limited.

If I am correct in assuming the potential conflict between individual values and institutional or professional goals, then we must recognize that in most instances in which librarians act courageously, they will do so without ever receiving formal support. If I take a stand against the director who is closing branches to save money to support the business collection, it is more likely that I will be considered politically naive than courageous and virtuous. The greater the struggle for resources within our communities and institutions, the more likely such compromises will be made.

We face a dilemma. Individual staff attitudes are the first ingredient to achieving the goal of effective access to information, but we exist in institutions that struggle for survival. Given the inherent conflicts between individuals and institutions, each one of us is bound up in an inescapable struggle to practice with virtue--with justice, with courage, and with honesty. We repeatedly seek ways to avoid compromising our commitment to providing access to information in the face of the enormous economic pressures all libraries face.

I have no conclusive solution to this dilemma, but I am heartened by statements such as those offered by F. William Summers in the opening essay that remind us of the moral and ethical basis of our professional beliefs. I am also heartened by the individuals we are recruiting to our profession.

In answer to the recent OLPR study of students in schools of library and information science, one of our students answered the question "Why did you choose this profession as a field of work?" in the following way: "Because providing information to people who want it is a good thing to do. Because libraries do not pollute, do not destroy, do not attempt to create wealth out of nothing. Because I am concerned that many people do not have access to information. Because I can justify libraries on moral and ethical grounds. And because I like to read and find things out."

We must nurture such attitudes and support one another that we might achieve justice within our profession.

Notes

1.   Leigh Estabrook, "Emerging Trends in Community Library Services," *Library Trends*, Fall 1979, 151-64.

2.   Margaret Kimmel, "Professional Strivings and the Orientation of Public Librarians toward Lower-Class Clients," diss., University of Pittsburgh, 1980 (microfilm).

3.   Ibid., 97.

4.   Ibid., 98.

5.   Leigh Stewart Estabrook, "Librarianship and Information Resource Management: Some Questions and Contradictions," *Journal of Education for Library and Information Science*, Summer 1986.

6.   Alasdair MacIntyre, *After Virtue*, 2d ed. (Notre Dame, Ind.: University of Notre Dame Press, 1984).

7.   Ibid., 193.

8.   Ibid., 191.

9.   Ibid., 192.

10.   Ibid.

11.   Ibid., 194.

Bibliography:
Suggested Additional Reading

The Need to Know

American Library Association. Commission on Freedom and Equality of Access to Information. *Freedom and Equality of Access to Information.* A Report to the American Library Association. Chicago: ALA, 1986.

Bezold, Clement, and Robert Olson. "The Information Millennium: Alternative Futures." *Insight* 4, no. 7 (July 1987):16-21.

The Need to Know: Citizen Responsibility in a Free Society. New York: The Field Foundation, April 1986.

The Government's Philosophy and Practice

OMB Perspective on Electronic Collection and Dissemination of Information

"Management of Federal Information Resources (OMB Circular No. A-130, Final publication)." *Federal Register* 50, no. 247 (24 December 1985):52730-52751; "Corrections," *Federal Register* 51, no. 3 (6 January 1986):461.

Office of Management and Budget, Circular No. A-76, 1983 (revised).

Paperwork Reduction Act, as amended, Title 44, *United States Code,* Section 3505(5).

Sprehe, J. Timothy. "Federal Policy on Information Access and Dissemination." *Information Society* 5 (1987):19-24.

_____. "OMB Circular No. A-130, The Management of Federal Information Resources: Its Origins and Impact." *Government Information Quarterly* 4 (1987):189-96.

Stokes, Judith E. "Federal Publication Cutbacks: Implications for Libraries." *Government Information Quarterly* 1, no. 1 (1984):49-57.

The Congressional Role

Brooks, Jack. "Government Information and New Technology: A Viewpoint." *Government Publications Review* 13 (1986):177-79.

Brown, George E., Jr. "Federal Information Policy: Protecting the Free Flow of Information." *Government Information Quarterly* 4 (1987):349-58.

_____. "Restricting Information: National Security versus Rights of Citizens." *ASIS Bulletin*, April 1982, 34-35.

U.S. Congress. Joint Committee on Printing, Ad Hoc Advisory Committee on Title 44 to the Joint Committee on Printing. *Federal Government Printing and Publishing: Policy Issues.* Washington, D.C.: GPO, 1979.

The Role of the Courts

Bolner, James. "The Reagan Administration versus the Joint Committee on Printing: Constitutional Reflections." *Government Publications Review* 12 (1985):105-18.

Hernon, Peter, and Charles R. McClure. *Public Access to Government Information: Issues, Trends, and Strategies.* Norwood, N.J.: Ablex Publishing Corporation, 1984.

Jones, Mary Gardiner. "Citizens' Rights to Information: The Role of Government." *Information Services & Use,* 1985, 37-47.

Levin, Marc A. "Access and Dissemination Issues Concerning Federal Government Information." *Special Libraries* 74 (April 1983):127-37.

The Private Sector's Philosophy and Role

The View from the Information Industry Association

Meeting Information Needs in the New Information Age. Washington, D.C.: Information Industry Association, 1983.

Smith, Diane. "The Commercialization and Privatization of Government Information." *Government Publications Review* 12 (1985):45-63.

Willard, Robert S., Donna A. Demac, and Allan Adler. "Whose Information Is It Anyway?" *Government Information Review* 13 (1986):323-35.

Through the Eyes of the Entrepreneur

Adler, James B. "Publishers, Libraries, and the Future Use of Government Information." *Government Publications Review* 9 (1982):87-90.

Freides, Thelma. "The Federal Information Controversy from and Economic Perspective." *College & Research Libraries*, September 1986, 425-37.

A Librarian's Perspective

Association of Research Libraries. "Access to Information: A Statement from the Association of Research Libraries." October 1985.

Council on Library Resources. "Scholarship, Research, and Access to Information: A Statement from the Council on Library Resources." January 1985.

National Commission on Libraries and Information Science. Public Sector/Private Sector Task Force. *Public Sector/Private Sector Interaction in Providing Information Services.* Washington, D.C.: GPO, February 1982.

Schuman, Patricia Glass. "Information Justice: A Review of the NCLIS Task Force Report: Public/Private Sector Interaction in Providing Information Services." *Library Journal*, 1 June 1982, 1060-66.

The Librarian and Information Specialist View

The Government Documents Depository System

American Library Association. "Less Access to Less Information By and About the U.S. Government, January 1981-June 1987." Reprinted in *Documents to the People* 15, no. 2 (June 1987):76-102: covers 1981-1986; 15, no. 3 (September 1987):162-68: covers January-June 1987.

Association of Research Libraries. *Technology & U.S. Government Information Policies: Catalysts for New Partnerships.* Report of the Task Force on Government Information in Electronic Format. Washington, D.C.: ARL, October 1987.

Bochnig, P.M. "Recent Literature on Government Information." *Government Publications Review* 12 (July/August 1985):345-59; 13 (March/April 1986):265-75; 13 (September/October 1986):617-29.

Fry, Bernard M. *Government Publications: Their Role in the National Program for Library and Information Services.* Washington, D.C.: NCLIS, 1978.

Harrison, James L. *100 GPO Years, 1861-1961.* Washington, D.C.: GPO, 1961.

Schwarzkopf, LeRoy C. "Depository Libraries and Public Access." In *Collection Development and Public Access of Government Documents.* Westport, Conn.: Meckler Publishing, 1982, 7-33.

U.S. General Accounting Office. *Depository Librarians' Views on GPO's Administration of the Depository Library Program.* Washington, D.C.: GAO, 1984.

Williams, Wiley J. *Subject Guide to Major United States Government Publications.* 2d ed. Chicago: ALA, 1987.

Resource Sharing through Networking

Atkinson, Hugh C. "Atkinson on Networks." *American Libraries*, June 1987, 432-36.

Avram, Henriette D. "Current Issues in Networking." *Journal of Academic Librarianship* 12, no. 4 (September 1986):205-9.

Dowlin, Ken. "Access to Information and Knowledge: A Human Right?" In *BARC Notes*, February 1988, 9-14.

Potter, William. "Readers in Search of Authors: The Changing Face of the Middleman." *Wilson Library Bulletin*, April 1986, 20-23.

Ptacek, Bill, and Darlene Roby. "Reality Clears Away the Clouds: The Current Technology and Resource Sharing." *Library Journal*, 1 February 1988, 40-41.

Rochell, Carlton C. "The Next Decade: Distributed Access to Information." *Library Journal*, 1 February 1987, 42-48.

Sloan, Bernard G. "Resource Sharing Among Academic Libraries: The LCS Experience." *Journal of Academic Librarianship* 12, no. 1 (March 1986):26-29.

Trezza, Alphonse F. "Equal Opportunity of Access: A Responsibility and a Challenge." *Government Publications Review* 13 (1986):49-54.

The Fee or Free Dilemma

Berry, John. "Practice and Principle: The Fee Example." *Library Journal* 113, no. 2 (1 February 1988):4.

Drake, Miriam A. "User Fees--Aid or Obstacle to Access." In *1984 Conference for Public Libraries: Managing Information--A National Imperative*. Tallahassee, Fla.: Florida State University, 1985, 23-27.

"Fees for Library Service: Current Practice and Future Policy." *Collection Building* 8, no. 1 (1986), entire issue.

Kranach, Nancy. "Fees for Library Service: They Are Not Inevitable." *Library Journal* 105 (1 May 1980):1048-51.

National Commission on Libraries and Information Science. *The Role of Fees in Supporting Library and Information Services in Public and Academic Libraries*. Washington, D.C.: NCLIS, April 1985.

Van House, Nancy A. *Public Library User Fees: The Use and Finance of Public Libraries*. Westport, Conn.: Greenwood Press, 1983.

Waldhart, Thomas J., and Trudi Bellardo. "User Fees in Publicly Funded Libraries." *Advances in Librarianship* 9 (1979):31-61.

The Needs of the Many Publics

Scholars, Youth, and the General Public

Battin, Patricia. "The Library: Center of the Restructured University." In *Colleges Enter the Information Society: 1983-84 Current Issues in Higher Education*, 25-31. Washington, D.C.: American Association for Higher Education, 1984.

Govan, James F. "The Creeping Invisible Hand: Entrepreneurial Librarianship." *Library Journal* (January 1988):35-38.

"Information in the Economy" (special section). *Bulletin of the American Society for Information Science* 14, no.3 (February/March 1988):12-25.

Lambert, Richard D., et al. *Beyond Growth: The Next Stage in Language and Area Studies*. Washington, D.C.: Association of American Universities, April 1984. Especially chapter 6, "Library and Information Resources," 232-59.

Nickerson, Raymond S. *Using Computers: The Human Factors of Information Systems*. Cambridge, Mass.: MIT Press, 1986.

"Reading Old and New." *Daedalus* (Journal of the American Academy of Arts and Sciences) 112, no.1 (Winter 1983), entire issue.

Removing or Neutralizing Barriers

Illiteracy and Aliteracy

Goodrum, Charles A., and Helen Dalrymple. "Illiteracy in the United States." In *Books in Our Future*. Washington, D.C.: Library of Congress, 1987,40-50.

Harman, David. *Illiteracy: A National Dilemma*. New York: Cambridge Book Co., 1987.

Heiser, Jane-Carol. *Literacy Resources: An Annotated Check List for Tutors and Librarians*. Baltimore, Md.: Enoch Proatt Free Library, 1983.

Kozol, Jonathan. *Illiterate America*. New York: Anchor Press/Doubleday, 1985.

Lyman, Helen Huguenor. *Literacy and the Nation's Libraries*. Chicago: American Library Association, 1977.

Technologies and Barriers to Information Access

Berman, Sanford. "Added Entries: The Cataloging Mystique--and Automation." *HCL Cataloging Bulletin*, no. 32 (January/February 1978):15-22.

_____. "1. Libraries--Forecasts. 2. Elitism in Librarianship." *Library Journal* 105 (1 January 1980):23-27.

Cotter, Eithne, and Emily McCarty. "Technology for the Handicapped: Kurzweil and Viewscan." *Library Hi Tech* 1 (Winter 1983):63-67.

Demas, Samuel G. "Freedom of Access to Information in Machine Readable Form: The Librarians Role." In *Energies for Transition*. Proceedings of the Fourth National Conference of the Association of College and Research Libraries. Baltimore, Md.: ACRL, 1986.

Konoshima, Sumiye. "Barriers and Prospects for Transborder Data Flow." *Bulletin of the American Society for Information Science* 13 (April/May 1987):32-33.

Malinconico, S. Michael. "Hearing the Resistance." *Library Journal* 108 (15 January 1983):111-13.

_____. "Listening to the Resistance." *Library Journal* 108 (15 February 1983):353-55.

Markey, Karen. "Barriers to Effective Use of Online Catalogs." In *Online Catalogs, Online Reference*. Chicago, Ill.: American Library Association, 1984.

Potter, William Gray. "Libraries, Computing Centers, and Freedom of Access." *Journal of Academic Librarianship* 13:298.

Redfern, Brian. "Dinosaurs to Crush Flies: Computer Catalogues, Classification and Other Barriers to Library Use." *Brio* 21 (Spring/Summer 1984):4-8.

U.S. Congress. Joint Committee on Printing, Ad Hoc Committee on Depository Library Access to Federal Automated Data Bases. *Provision of Federal Government Publications in Electronic Format to Depository Libraries*. Washington, D.C.: GPO, 1984.

Staff Attitudes: Conflicting Values

Daniel, Evelyn. "Librarians as Information Managers." In *Public Libraries and the Challenges of the Next Two Decades*. Littleton, Colo.: Libraries Unlimited, 1985, 244-50.

Estabrook, Leigh S. "Librarianship and Information Resources Management: Some Questions and Contradictions." *Journal of Education for Library and Information Science* 27, no.1 (Summer 1986):3-11.

Fine, Sara. "Interpersonal Relationships in a Technological Age." In *Public Libraries and the Challenges of the Next Two Decades*. Littleton, Colo.: Libraries Unlimited, 1985, 199-207.

Hentoff, Nat. "The Day the Library Almost Disappeared." *Village Voice* 33, no. 5 (2 February 1988):36.

McIntyre, Alisdair. *After Virtue: A Study in Moral Theory*. 2nd ed. Notre Dame, Indiana: Notre Dame University Press, 1984.

White, Herbert S. "Librarians and Information Managers." *Library Journal* 112, no. 4 (4 March 1987):52-53.

_____. "Technical Excellence Versus Service Orientation." In *Public Libraries and the Challenges of the Next Two Decades*. Littleton, Colo.: Libraries Unlimited, 1985, 235-43.